SCHOLASTIC

25 Complex Text Passages to Meet the Common Core

Literature and Informational Texts

Grade 3

by Martin Lee and Marcia Miller

NEW YORK ● TORONTO ● LONDON ● AUCKLAND ● SYDNEY
MEXICO CITY ● NEW DELHI ● HONG KONG ● BUENOS AIRES

Teaching *Resources*

Cover design: Scott Davis
Interior design: Kathy Massaro

Interior illustrations: Teresa Anderko, Delana Bettoli, Maxie Chambliss, Rusty Fletcher, James Graham Hale, and Mike Moran
© 2014 by Scholastic Inc.

Image credits: page 28 © Zack Frank/Shutterstock, Inc.; page 34 © Tom Reichner/Shutterstock, Inc.;
page 38 © JeffreyThompson/Big Stock Photo; page 40 © Jim Parkin/Shutterstock, Inc.; page 42 (top) © Solomon Butcher Collection/
Nebraska State Historical Society; page 42 (bottom) © Solomon Butcher Collection/Nebraska State Historical Society;
page 44 © Blinka/Shutterstock, Inc.; page 48 © SteveUnit4/Shutterstock, Inc.; page 58 © GlobalStock/iStockphoto; page 60 © NASA;
page 62 © 2happy/Shutterstock, Inc.; page 64 (top) © Randi Scott/Shutterstock, Inc.; page 64 (bottom) © calebphoto/iStockphoto;
page 68 © elina/Shutterstock, Inc.; page 74 (top) © FloridaStock/Shutterstock, Inc.; page 74 (bottom) © Jeff Banke/Shutterstock, Inc.

ISBN: 978-0-545-57709-0
Copyright © 2014 by Scholastic Inc.
All rights reserved.
Printed in the U.S.A.
Published by Scholastic Inc.

1 2 3 4 5 6 7 8 9 10   40   21 20 19 18 17 16 15 14

Contents

"To build a foundation for college and career readiness, students must read widely and deeply from among a broad range of high-quality, increasingly challenging literary and informational texts. Through extensive reading of stories, dramas, poems, and myths from diverse cultures and different time periods, students gain literary and cultural knowledge as well as familiarity with various text structures and elements. By reading texts in history/social studies, science, and other disciplines, students build a foundation of knowledge in these fields that will also give them the background to be better readers in all content areas. Students can only gain this foundation when the curriculum is intentionally and coherently structured to develop rich content knowledge within and across grades. Students also acquire the habits of reading independently and closely, which are essential to their future success."

—COMMON CORE STATE STANDARDS FOR ENGLISH LANGUAGE ARTS, JUNE 2010

25 Complex Text Passages to Meet the Common Core: Literature and Informational Texts—Grade 3 includes complex reading passages with companion comprehension question pages for teaching the two types of texts—Literature and Informational—covered in the Common Core State Standards (CCSS) for English Language Arts. The passages and lessons in this book address the rigorous expectations put forth by the CCSS "that students read increasingly complex texts through the grades." This book embraces nine of the ten CCSS College and Career Readiness Anchor Standards for Reading that inform solid instruction for literary and informational texts.

Anchor Standards for Reading

Key Ideas and Details

1. Read closely to determine what the text says explicitly and make logical inferences from it; cite specific textual evidence when writing or speaking to support conclusions drawn from the text.

2. Determine central ideas or themes of a text; summarize key supporting details and ideas.

3. Analyze how and why individuals, events, and ideas develop and interact throughout a text.

Craft and Structure

4. Interpret words and phrases as they are used in a text, including determining technical, connotative, and figurative meanings, and analyze how specific word choices shape meaning or tone.

5. Analyze the structure of texts, including how specific sentences, paragraphs, and larger portions of text relate to each other and the whole.

6. Assess how point of view or purpose shapes the content and style of a text.

Integration of Knowledge and Ideas

7. Integrate and evaluate content presented in diverse media and formats, including visually and quantitatively, as well as in words.

8. Delineate and evaluate the argument and specific claims in a text, including the validity of the reasoning as well as the relevance and sufficiency of the evidence.

Range of Reading and Level of Text Complexity

10. Read and comprehend complex literary and informational texts independently and proficiently.

The materials in this book also address the Foundational Standards for Reading, including skills in phonics, word recognition, and fluency as well as Language Standards, such as the conventions of standard English, knowledge of language, and vocabulary acquisition and use. In addition, students meet Writing Standards as they answer questions about the passages, demonstrating their ability to convey ideas coherently, clearly, and with support from the text. On page 12, you'll find a correlation chart that details how the 25 passages meet specific standards. This information can also be found with the teaching notes for each passage on pages 13–25.

About Text Complexity

The CCSS recommend that students tackle increasingly complex texts to develop and hone their skills and knowledge. Many factors contribute to the complexity of any text.

Text complexity is more intricate than a readability score alone reveals. Most formulas examine sentence length and structure and the number of difficult words. Each formula gives different weight to different factors. Other aspects of text complexity include coherence, organization, motivation, and any prior knowledge readers may bring.

A complex text can be relatively easy to decode, but if it examines complex issues or uses figurative language, the overall text complexity rises. By contrast, a text that uses unfamiliar words may be less daunting if readers can apply word-study skills and context clues effectively to determine meaning.

This triangular model used by the CCSS shows three distinct yet interrelated factors that contribute to text complexity.

CCSS Model of Text Complexity

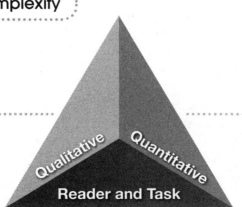

Qualitative measures consider the complexity of meaning or purpose, structure, language conventionality, and overall clarity.

Quantitative measures complexity in terms of word length and frequency, sentence length, and text cohesion. Lexile® algorithms rank this type of complexity on a numerical scale.

Reader and Task considerations refer to such variables as a student's motivation, knowledge, and experience brought to the text, and the purpose, complexity, and types of questions posed.

About the Passages

The 25 reproducible, one-page passages included in this book are divided into two categories. The first 9 passages represent literature (fiction) and are followed by 16 informational texts (nonfiction). Each grouping presents a variety of genres and forms, organizational structures, purposes, tones, and tasks. Consult the table of contents (page 3) to see the scope of genres, forms, and types of content-area texts. The passages within each category are arranged in order of Lexile score (the quantitative measure), from lowest to highest, and fall within the Lexile score ranges recommended for third graders. The Lexile scores for grade 3, revised to reflect the more rigorous demands of the CCSS, range from 520 to 820. For more about determinations of complexity levels, see page 5 and pages 8–9.

Each passage appears on its own page beginning with the title, the genre or form of the passage, and an opening question to give students a focus to keep in mind as they read. Some passages also include visual elements, such as photographs, drawings, illustrations, or tables, as well as typical text elements, such as italics, boldface type, bulleted or numbered lists, subheadings, or sidebars.

The line numbers that appear to the left of each passage will help you and your students readily locate a specific line of text. For example, students might say, "I'm not sure how to pronounce the name here in line 6." They might also include line numbers to identify text evidence when they answer questions about the piece. For example: "The author says in lines 11–13 that…"

The passages are stand-alone texts and can be used in any order you choose. Feel free to assign passages to individuals, small groups, or the entire class, as best suits your teaching style. However, it's a good idea to preview each passage before you assign it, to ensure that your students have the skills needed to complete it successfully. (See page 10 for a close-reading routine to model for students.)

About the After-Reading Question Pages

The Common Core standards suggest that assessment should involve "text-dependent questions." Questions constructed to meet this demand guide students to cite evidence from the text. They fall into three broad categories: 1) Key Ideas and Details, 2) Craft and Structure, and 3) Integration of Knowledge and Ideas. According to the standards, responses should include claims supported by the text, connections to informational or literary elements found within the

25 Complex Text Passages to Meet the Common Core: Literature and Informational Texts, Grade 3 © 2014 by Scholastic Teaching Resources

text explicitly or by logical implication, and age-appropriate analyses of themes or topics.

Following each passage is a reproducible page with five text-dependent comprehension questions for students to answer after reading. Two are multiple-choice questions that call for a single response and a brief text-based explanation to justify that choice. The other questions are open response items. These address a range of comprehension strategies and skills. Students can revisit the passage to find the evidence they need to answer each question. All questions share the goal of ensuring that students engage in close reading of the text, grasp its key ideas, and provide text-based evidence in their answers. In addition, the questions are formatted to reflect the types of questions that will be asked on standardized tests. The questions generally proceed from easier to more complex:

✳ The **least challenging** questions call for basic understanding and recall of details. They involve referencing the text verbatim or paraphrasing it. This kind of question might also ask students to identify a supporting detail an author did or did not include when making a persuasive argument.

✳ The **mid-level** questions call upon students to use mental processes beyond basic recall. To answer these questions, students may need to use context clues to unlock the meaning of unfamiliar words and phrases (including figurative language), classify or compare information, make inferences, distinguish facts from opinions, or make predictions. Such a question might also ask students to summarize the main idea(s) of a passage.

✳ The **deeper** questions focus on understanding that goes beyond the text. Students may need to recognize the author's tone and purpose, make inferences about the entire passage, or use logic to make predictions. This kind of question might even call upon students to determine why an author began or ended the passage as he or she did.

You may find it useful to have students reference line numbers from the passage for efficiency and clarity when they formulate answers. They can also refer to the line numbers during class discussions. Provide additional paper so students have ample space to write complete and thorough answers.

An answer key (pages 76–80) includes sample answers based on textual evidence and specific line numbers from the passage that support the answers. You might want to review answers with the whole class. This approach provides opportunities for discussion, comparison, extension, reinforcement, and correlation to other skills and lessons in your current plans. Your observations can direct the kinds of review and reinforcement you may want to add to subsequent lessons.

About the Teaching Notes

Each passage in this book is supported by a set of teaching notes found on pages 13–25.

In the left column, you will see the following features for each set of teaching notes.

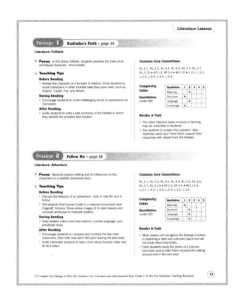

✳ Grouping (**Literature** or **Informational Text**) and the genre or form of the piece.

✳ **Focus** statement describing the essential purpose of the passage, its main features, areas of emphasis, and what students will gain by reading it.

✳ **Teaching Tips** to help you motivate, support, and guide students before, during, and after reading. These easy-to-use suggestions are by no means exhaustive, and you may choose to add or substitute your own ideas or strategies.

- **Before Reading** tips include ways to introduce a passage, explain a genre, present a topic, discuss a format, introduce key vocabulary, or put a theme in context. A tip may suggest how to engage prior knowledge, connect with similar materials in other curriculum areas, or build motivation.

- **During Reading** tips offer possible procedures to help students work through the text, ideas for highlighting key words or concepts, suggestions for graphic organizers, and so on.

- **After Reading** tips provide follow-up questions, discussion topics, extension activities, further readings, or writing assignments linked to the text.

In the right column, are the essential CCSS connections for the passage sorted according to the specific sections of the document: **RL** (Reading Standards for Literature) or **RI** (Reading Standards for Informational Text), **RF** (Reading Standards: Foundational Skills), **W** (Writing Standards), and **L** (Language Standards). The CCSS chart on page 12 provides the correlations for the entire book at a glance and a URL for the CCSS website where you can find the specific wording of each skill.

Under the essential CCSS connections, you will find a **Complexity Index**, which offers analytical information about the passage based on the three aspects of text complexity, briefly summarized on the next page.

❋ **Quantitative** value, represented by a Lexile score.

❋ **Qualitative** rating, which appears in a matrix that presents four aspects of this measure:

- **Meaning** for literary texts (single level of meaning ↔ multiple levels of meaning) or **Purpose** for informational texts (explicitly stated purpose ↔ implicit purpose)

- **Structure** (simple ↔ complex organization; simple ↔ complex graphics)

- **Language** (literal ↔ figurative; clear ↔ ambiguous; familiar ↔ unusual; conversational ↔ formal)

- **Knowledge** (life experience; content expectations; cultural or literary background needed)

Each of the above aspects are ranked from 1 to 5, briefly summarized, as follows:

1	2	3	4	5
Simple, clear text; accessible language, ideas, and/or structure	Mostly linear with explicit meaning/ purpose; clear structure; moderate vocabulary; assumes some knowledge	May have more than one meaning/ purpose; some figurative language; more demanding structure, syntax, language, and/ or vocabulary; assumes some knowledge	Multiple meanings/ purposes possible; more sophisticated syntax, structure, language, and/ or vocabulary; assumes much knowledge	May require inference and/ or synthesis; complex structure, syntax, language, and/ or vocabulary; assumes extensive knowledge

❋ **Reader and Task** considerations comprise two or more bulleted points. Ideas relating to the reader appear first, followed by specific suggestions for a text-based task. Reader and Task considerations also appear embedded within the teaching notes as well as in the guiding question that opens each passage and in the comprehension questions. Keep in mind that Reader and Task considerations are the most variable of the three measures of text complexity. Reader issues relate to such broad concerns as prior knowledge and experience, cognitive abilities, reading skills, motivation by and engagement with the text, and content and/or theme concerns. Tasks are typically questions to answer, ideas to discuss, or activities to help students navigate and analyze the text, understand key ideas, and deepen comprehension. The same task may be stimulating for some students but daunting to others. Because you know your students best, use your judgment to adjust and revise tasks as appropriate.

Teaching Routine to Support Close Reading

Complex texts become more accessible to readers who are able to use various strategies during the reading process. One of the best ways to scaffold students through this process is to model a close-reading routine.

✳ **Preview the text.** Help students learn to identify clues about the meaning, purpose, or goal of the text. They can first read the title and the guiding question that precedes the passage. In literary texts, students can scan for characters' names and clues about setting and time frame. In informational texts, students can use features such as paragraph subheadings and supporting photos, illustrations, or other graphics to get a sense of the organization and purpose.

✳ **Quick-read to get the gist.** Have students do a "run-through" individual reading of the passage to get a sense of it. The quick-read technique can also help students identify areas of confusion or problem vocabulary. You can liken this step to scanning a new store to get a sense of how it is set up, what products it sells, and how you can find what you need.

✳ **Read closely.** Next, have students read the same piece again, this time with an eye to unlocking its deeper meaning or purpose. For most students, this is the time to use sticky notes, highlighter pens, margin notes, or graphic organizers to help them work their way through the important parts of the text. You might provide text-related graphic organizers, such as T-charts, compare/contrast and Venn diagrams, character and concept maps, cause-and-effect charts, or evidence/conclusion tables.

✳ **Respond to the text.** Now it's time for students to pull their ideas together and for you to assess their understanding. This may involve summarizing, reading aloud, holding group discussions, debates, or answering written questions. When you assign the after-reading question pages, suggest that students reread questions as needed before they attempt an answer. Encourage them to return to the text as well. Remind students to provide text-based evidence as part of every answer. Finally, consider with students the big ideas of a piece, its message, lesson, or purpose, and think about how to extend learning.

Above all, use the passages and teaching materials in this book to inspire students to become mindful readers—readers who delve deeply into a text to get the most out of it. Help your students recognize that reading is much more than just decoding all the words. Guide them to dig in, think about ideas, determine meaning, and grasp messages.

The following page presents two copies of a reproducible, six-step guide to mindful reading. It is intended as a reusable prompt. Students can keep it at hand to help them recall, apply, and internalize close-reading strategies whenever they read.

How to Be A Mindful Reader

Preview the text.
- What might it be about?

Read carefully.
- Stop to think as you read.
- Monitor your understanding.

Read again.
- You might notice new information.

Take notes.
- Circle the hard words.
- Write questions you may have.

Summarize.
- Jot down the main ideas.
- List the big events in order.

Think about it.
- What's the message?
- What ideas stand out?

How to Be A Mindful Reader

Preview the text.
- What might it be about?

Read carefully.
- Stop to think as you read.
- Monitor your understanding.

Read again.
- You might notice new information.

Take notes.
- Circle the hard words.
- Write questions you may have.

Summarize.
- Jot down the main ideas.
- List the big events in order.

Think about it.
- What's the message?
- What ideas stand out?

Connections to the Common Core State Standards

As shown in the chart below, the teaching resources in this book will help you meet many of the reading, writing, and language standards for grade 3 outlined in the CCSS. For details on these standards, visit the CCSS website: www.corestandards.org/the-standards/.

Passage	RL.3.1	RL.3.2	RL.3.3	RL.3.4	RL.3.5	RL.3.6	RL.3.7	RL.3.10	RI.3.1	RI.3.2	RI.3.3	RI.3.4	RI.3.5	RI.3.6	RI.3.7	RI.3.8	RI.3.10	RF.3.3	RF.3.4	W.3.10	L.3.1	L.3.2	L.3.3	L.3.4	L.3.5	L.3.6
	Reading: Literature								Reading: Informational Text									Reading: Foundational Skills		Writing	Language					
1	●	●	●	●	●		●	●										●	●	●	●	●	●	●	●	●
2	●	●	●	●	●	●	●	●										●	●	●	●	●	●	●	●	●
3	●	●	●	●	●		●	●										●	●	●	●	●	●	●	●	●
4	●	●	●	●	●	●		●										●	●	●	●	●	●	●	●	●
5	●	●	●	●	●		●	●										●	●	●	●	●	●	●	●	●
6	●	●	●	●	●		●	●										●	●	●	●	●	●	●	●	●
7	●	●	●		●		●	●										●	●	●	●	●	●	●	●	●
8	●	●	●	●	●	●		●										●	●	●	●	●	●	●	●	●
9	●	●	●	●	●		●	●										●	●	●	●	●	●	●	●	●
10									●	●	●	●		●		●	●	●	●	●	●	●	●	●	●	●
11									●	●	●	●	●		●	●	●	●		●	●	●	●	●	●	●
12									●	●	●				●	●	●	●	●	●	●	●	●	●	●	●
13									●	●	●	●			●	●	●	●	●	●	●	●	●	●	●	●
14									●	●	●	●		●	●	●	●	●	●	●	●	●	●	●	●	●
15									●	●	●	●	●		●	●		●		●	●	●	●	●	●	●
16									●	●		●		●	●	●	●	●	●	●	●	●	●	●	●	●
17									●	●	●	●	●	●	●	●	●	●	●	●	●	●	●	●	●	●
18									●	●	●				●	●	●	●	●	●	●	●	●	●	●	●
19									●	●	●				●	●	●	●	●	●	●	●	●	●	●	●
20									●	●	●	●	●		●	●	●	●	●	●	●	●	●	●	●	●
21									●	●	●	●	●		●	●	●	●	●	●	●	●	●	●	●	●
22									●	●	●	●	●		●	●	●	●	●	●	●	●	●	●	●	●
23									●	●	●	●			●	●	●	●	●	●	●	●	●		●	●
24									●	●	●	●			●	●	●	●	●	●	●		●		●	●
25									●	●	●	●	●	●	●	●	●	●	●	●		●	●	●	●	●

Passage 1 — Kadimba's Field • page 26

Literature: Folktale

▶ **Focus** In this Bantu folktale, students examine the traits of an archetypal character—the trickster.

▶ **Teaching Tips**

Before Reading
- Review the character of a trickster in folklore. Invite students to recall characters in other trickster tales they have read, such as Anansi, Coyote, Fox, and Iktomi.

During Reading
- Encourage students to circle challenging words or expressions for discussion.

After Reading
- Invite students to write a plot summary of the folktale in which they identify the problem and solution.

Common Core Connections

RL.3.1, RL.3.2, RL.3.3, RL.3.4, RL.3.5, RL.3.7, RL.3.10 • RF.3.3, RF.3.4 • W.3.10 • L.3.1, L.3.2, L.3.3, L.3.4, L.3.5, L.3.6

Complexity Index

Quantitative: Lexile 580

Qualitative	1	2	3	4	5
Meaning		✵			
Structure	✵				
Language		✵			
Knowledge	✵				

Reader & Task

- The labor-intensive tasks involved in farming may be unfamiliar to students.
- Ask students to answer this question: *Was Kadimba really lazy?* Have them support their responses with details from the folktale.

Passage 2 — Follow Me • page 28

Literature: Adventure

▶ **Focus** Students explore setting and its influences on the characters in a realistic adventure story.

▶ **Teaching Tips**

Before Reading
- Discuss the features of an adventure—both in real life and in fiction.
- Tell students that Sunset Crater is a national monument near Flagstaff, Arizona. Show online images of its stark beauty and unusual landscape to motivate readers.

During Reading
- Help readers notice vivid descriptions, precise language, and emotional clues.

After Reading
- Encourage students to compare and contrast the two main characters, then infer how each felt upon leaving the lava tube.
- Invite interested students to learn more about Sunset Crater and its lava tubes.

Common Core Connections

RL.3.1, RL.3.2, RL.3.3, RL.3.4, RL.3.5, RL.3.6, RL.3.7, RL.3.10 • RF.3.3, RF.3.4 • W.3.10 • L.3.1, L.3.2, L.3.3, L.3.4, L.3.5, L.3.6

Complexity Index

Quantitative: Lexile 630

Qualitative	1	2	3	4	5
Meaning	✵				
Structure		✵			
Language		✵			
Knowledge		✵			

Reader & Task

- Most readers will recognize the feelings involved in exploring a dark and unknown place but will not know about lava tubes.
- Have students study the photo of a volcanic lava tube cave to help them visualize the setting around and in the lava tube.

Literature: Humorous Stories

▶ **Focus** Students must understand puns, slang, homophones, and other forms of wordplay to find the humor in two short humorous stories.

▶ **Teaching Tips**

Before Reading
● Define a *pun* as a joke or "play on words" whose purpose is to entertain. Explain that some puns rely on a multiple-meaning word or a homophone used unexpectedly. Review what homophones are, and how they can be confusing. Discuss this example: *Time flies like the wind. Fruit flies like the banana.*

During Reading
● Have students identify the key words or phrases that comprise the punch lines.
● Encourage students to read each joke aloud using good expression, as if they were a stand-up comic.

After Reading
● Extend by having students read more examples of puns, double-entendres, malapropisms, and other forms of wordplay.

Common Core Connections

RL.3.1, RL.3.2, RL.3.3, RL.3.4, RL.3.5, RL.3.7, RL.3.10 • RF.3.3, RF.3.4 • W.3.10 • L.3.1, L.3.2, L.3.3, L.3.4, L.3.5, L.3.6

Complexity Index

Quantitative: Lexile 660

Qualitative	1	2	3	4	5
Meaning			✳		
Structure	✳				
Language			✳		
Knowledge		✳			

Reader & Task

● Some students may not know the expression that is reversed in the first joke, or some of the slang terms used in the second joke.
● Guide students in deconstructing the punch lines in line 18 and lines 26–28 to ensure comprehension.

Literature: Realistic Fiction

▶ **Focus** Students must read between the lines to draw inferences about the actions of the characters in this story.

▶ **Teaching Tips**

Before Reading
● Remind students that writers often tell a story through actions rather than by giving detailed descriptions.

During Reading
● Suggest that readers jot down observations or comments about Inez, Lupe, and Tiger.
● Encourage students to visualize the setting and how Tiger moves through it.

After Reading
● Extend by inviting students to illustrate key moments in the story or rewrite it from Tiger's point of view.

Common Core Connections

RL.3.1, RL.3.2, RL.3.3, RL.3.4, RL.3.5, RL.3.6, RL.3.10 • RF.3.3, RF.3.4 • W.3.10 • L.3.1, L.3.2, L.3.3, L.3.4, L.3.5, L.3.6

Complexity Index

Quantitative: Lexile 670

Qualitative	1	2	3	4	5
Meaning			✳		
Structure	✳				
Language		✳			
Knowledge	✳				

Reader & Task

● Many readers will be motivated by a story about people and a clever cat.
● Have students describe the personality of each character, retell the events of the story, and analyze how the characters treated each other.

Literature: Tall Tale

▶ **Focus** This tall tale from Oregon helps students recognize the common features of a tall tale.

▶ **Teaching Tips**

Before Reading
- Discuss the typical features of tall tales (exaggeration, humor, absurdity, folksy language).

During Reading
- Guide readers to circle folksy language or peculiarities that indicate this is a tall tale.

After Reading
- Challenge students to write a 20-word summary of this tale. Guide them to choose their words carefully and to address the "5Ws": *Who? What? Where? Why? When?*

Common Core Connections

RL.3.1, RL.3.2, RL.3.3, RL.3.4, RL.3.5, RL.3.7, RL.3.10 • RF.3.3, RF.3.4 • W.3.10 • L.3.1, L.3.2, L.3.3, L.3.4, L.3.5, L.3.6

Complexity Index

Quantitative:
Lexile 680

Qualitative	1	2	3	4	5
Meaning		❋			
Structure		❋			
Language		❋			
Knowledge			❋		

Reader & Task

- Readers who lack prior knowledge about fishing may have difficulty grasping the oddities in this tall tale.
- Have students determine who tells this tale, and explain how they know.

Literature: Fable

▶ **Focus** This retelling of an Aesop fable lets readers explore a problem-and-solution structure and challenges them to understand its moral.

▶ **Teaching Tips**

Before Reading
- Review the features of a typical fable, including animal characters, simple language, brevity, a problem and its solution, and a moral.

During Reading
- Tell readers to pause after each paragraph to write a one-sentence summary of it.

After Reading
- Invite students to investigate the scientific concept of displacement that forms the basis of this story. Pour a small amount of water in a clear bottle with a narrow neck. Then have students drop in pebbles one by one and observe what happens to the water level.

Common Core Connections

RL.3.1, RL.3.2, RL.3.3, RL.3.4, RL.3.5, RL.3.7, RL.3.10 • RF.3.3, RF.3.4 • W.3.10 • L.3.1, L.3.2, L.3.3, L.3.4, L.3.5, L.3.6

Complexity Index

Quantitative:
Lexile 690

Qualitative	1	2	3	4	5
Meaning		❋			
Structure	❋				
Language		❋			
Knowledge			❋		

Reader & Task

- Most readers will be engaged by the crow's problem and amazed by her ingenious scientific solution.
- To check for comprehension, have students discuss how the moral follows from the story.

Literature: Myth

▶ **Focus** Students analyze the character traits of an important god in Norse mythology.

▶ **Teaching Tips**

Before Reading
- Review the nature of mythology and mythological figures.
- Clarify that the term *Norse* refers to early Scandinavian peoples and their culture. Identify the modern Scandinavian nations on a world map.

During Reading
- As students read, model the authentic pronunciations of the Norse names: Odin (*OH-din*), Asgard (*OZ-gard*), Hugin (*HYUG-in*), and Munin (*MYUN-in*).

After Reading
- Tell students that another nickname for Odin is *Raven God*. Discuss how details of this piece support that moniker. Extend by inviting students to suggest other nicknames for Odin, based on this piece.

Common Core Connections

RL.3.1, RL.3.2, RL.3.3, RL.3.4, RL.3.5, RL.3.7, RL.3.10 • RF.3.3, RF.3.4 • W.3.10 • L.3.1, L.3.2, L.3.3, L.3.4, L.3.5, L.3.6

Complexity Index

Quantitative:
Lexile 710

Qualitative	1	2	3	4	5
Meaning		✳			
Structure	✳				
Language		✳			
Knowledge		✳			

Reader & Task

- Many readers will enjoy learning about mythical figures and their superhuman powers.
- Encourage readers to generate a character map for Odin using words from the piece.

Literature: Mystery

▶ **Focus** This mystery challenges readers to infer the cause of an unexplained event.

▶ **Teaching Tips**

Before Reading
- Review the elements of a mystery.
- Present the idea of a boom town and discuss why many boom towns eventually go bust.

During Reading
- Invite students to describe how the photo serves as a context clue for visualizing the setting and understanding evocative details in the text.

After Reading
- Guide students to revisit the piece to identify clues the author used to hint at the explanation of the mystery. Then have students share their responses to question 4 (page 41) to explain what really happened.

Common Core Connections

RL.3.1, RL.3.2, RL.3.3, RL.3.4, RL.3.5, RL.3.6, RL.3.7, RL.3.10 • RF.3.3, RF.3.4 • W.3.10 • L.3.1, L.3.2, L.3.3, L.3.4, L.3.5, L.3.6

Complexity Index

Quantitative:
Lexile 760

Qualitative	1	2	3	4	5
Meaning			✳		
Structure		✳			
Language			✳		
Knowledge			✳		

Reader & Task

- Most students enjoy a mystery, especially if it is a bit scary!
- Have students discuss the following question: *What clues can you point out in this story that hint something scary might happen?*

Literature: Historical Fiction

▶ **Focus** Students use visualizing and inferencing skills to understand aspects of pioneer life.

▶ **Teaching Tips**

Before Reading
- Engage prior knowledge of pioneer life and the challenges of homesteading.

During Reading
- As they read, encourage students to examine the photos and use them as an aid in comprehension.
- Guide readers to jot notes in the margin about unfamiliar words or phrases, questions they may have about the setting or characters, or ideas to explore further.

After Reading
- Encourage students to discuss how and why every member of the family takes part in settling in.

Common Core Connections

RL.3.1, RL.3.2, RL.3.3, RL.3.4, RL.3.5, RL.3.7, RL.3.10 • RF.3.3, RF.3.4 • W.3.10 • L.3.1, L.3.2, L.3.3, L.3.4, L.3.5, L.3.6

Complexity Index

Quantitative:
Lexile 820

Qualitative	1	2	3	4	5
Meaning			✳		
Structure		✳			
Language			✳		
Knowledge				✳	

Reader & Task

- Students who may be acquainted with tales of pioneer life may know little about sod homes.
- Have students answer the question that precedes the passage by pointing to evidence in the text.

Passage 10 — Gary's Tuba • page 44

Informational Text: Interview/Diagram

▶ **Focus** Students gather new information from an interview presented in a question-and-answer format as well as a labeled diagram.

▶ **Teaching Tips**

Before Reading

- If possible, play several audio clips of tuba music (or a video of a tuba player in action). Invite students to respond to the sound and tone of the tuba.
- Review what an interview is. Then guide students to notice the question-and-answer structure and how it differs from other types of writing. Also have them think about how the person asking the questions might prepare in advance to get the best information.

During Reading

- Point out text features used in the interview: names in boldface, questions in italics, and answers in regular type. Discuss how these features help distinguish between the interview participants.
- Tell students to highlight any music terms that need clarification and to use the diagram to help them visualize the instrument and its parts.
- Discuss the purpose of the sidebar and the labeled diagram.

After Reading

- Encourage students to brainstorm a list of additional questions to ask about the tuba. If possible, invite a guest who plays the tuba to answer them or have students research the answers on their own.

Common Core Connections

RI.3.1, RI.3.2, RI.3.3, RI.3.4, RI.3.5, RI.3.7, RI.3.8, RI.3.10 • RF.3.3, RF.3.4 • W.3.10 • L.3.1, L.3.2, L.3.3, L.3.4, L.3.5, L.3.6

Complexity Index

Quantitative: Lexile 520

Qualitative	1	2	3	4	5
Purpose		✻			
Structure				✻	
Language		✻			
Knowledge			✻		

Reader & Task

- Students may be unfamiliar with the tuba—a lesser-known musical instrument.
- Have students evaluate each interview question for the kind of information it elicits.

Passage 11 — Wash and Dry • page 46

Informational Text: Procedural/Sign

▶ **Focus** In this procedural piece, students read ordered lists to understand how to complete a multi-step task.

▶ **Teaching Tips**

Before Reading

- Engage prior knowledge about doing the family laundry. Discuss sorting clothes by color or fabric, choosing washing and drying temperatures, and length of drying time.
- Point out different text features on the sign (boldface subheadings, numbered lists of steps, words in all capital letters, price list). Discuss how these features help to guide the reader.

During Reading

- Have students pause after each step to ensure comprehension. Encourage them to make connections among the steps.
- Ask students why it's important to read each set of instructions completely before washing or drying the clothes.

After Reading

- Invite students to come up with word problems similar to the one in question 4 (page 47) for classmates to solve.

Common Core Connections

RI.3.1, RI.3.2, RI.3.3, RI.3.4, RI.3.5, RI.3.7, RI.3.8, RI.3.10 • RF.3.3, RF.3.4 • W.3.10 • L.3.1, L.3.2, L.3.3, L.3.4, L.3.5, L.3.6

Complexity Index

Quantitative: Lexile 530

Qualitative	1	2	3	4	5
Purpose	✻				
Structure			✻		
Language		✻			
Knowledge	✻				

Reader & Task

- Students may not realize how many steps are involved in doing laundry.
- To help students better appreciate why the text is broken down into parts and sequential steps, ask: *How would the outcome change if the steps were not in order?*

Informational Text: Physical Science Article/Diagram

▶ **Focus** Using text and a labeled diagram, students connect and synthesize ideas to understand a common scientific phenomenon.

▶ **Teaching Tips**

Before Reading
● Engage prior knowledge about rainbows. Inform students that they will be reading an article about the science behind rainbows.

During Reading
● Tell students to highlight key sentences or phrases that help them determine the main idea of each paragraph.
● Encourage students to use the sidebar and the diagram as aids in understanding the text.

After Reading
● Guide students in synthesizing the information in the article to understand more about how rainbows form. Help them understand that water droplets in the air or mist from a hose act as tiny prisms to refract light.
● Extend by performing simple light refraction observations using prisms.

Common Core Connections

RI.3.1, RI.3.2, RI.3.3, RI.3.4, RI.3.5, RI.3.7, RI.3.8, RI.3.10 • RF.3.3, RF.3.4 • W.3.10 • L.3.1, L.3.2, L.3.3, L.3.4, L.3.5, L.3.6

Complexity Index

Quantitative: Lexile 550

Qualitative	1	2	3	4	5
Purpose			✳		
Structure				✳	
Language			✳		
Knowledge			✳		

Reader & Task

● Most students have seen rainbows but may have difficulty comprehending the scientific principles that cause them to appear.
● Have students explain what a rainbow is and tell what attributes all rainbows share.

Informational Text: Dictionary Entry

▶ **Focus** Students examine a typical dictionary entry and use it to determine which of the given meanings fits a word used in context.

▶ **Teaching Tips**

Before Reading
● Present a list of common multiple-meaning words, such as *grip*, *tie*, *mold*, or *feed*. Invite students to make up sentences for each meaning of these words.
● Review what students know about a dictionary entry, including the kind of information given and the way details are presented and organized.

During Reading
● Before students read lines 10–25, discuss the format of the dictionary entry. Help them identify the kind of information presented, and the different styles used to organize the details.
● Explain to students that meanings are usually listed from most to least common.
● Encourage students to read all parts of each definition to ensure that they can distinguish its meaning from the others and to understand its use in the sample sentences.

After Reading
● Provide dictionaries to pairs of students. Present sentences that feature a multiple-meaning word. Have pairs determine which dictionary meaning fits each usage.

Common Core Connections

RI.3.1, RI.3.2, RI.3.4, RI.3.5, RI.3.7, RI.3.8, RI.3.10 • RF.3.3, RF.3.4 • W.3.10 • L.3.1, L.3.2, L.3.3, L.3.4, L.3.5, L.3.6

Complexity Index

Quantitative: Lexile 580

Qualitative	1	2	3	4	5
Purpose			✳		
Structure			✳		
Language		✳			
Knowledge		✳			

Reader & Task

● Students may not have had sufficient practice using a dictionary.
● Have students summarize how to use a dictionary to find the appropriate meaning of a word that has more than one meaning.

Passage 14 Healthy and Crispy • page 52

Informational Text: Procedural/Recipe

▶ **Focus** Students use text elements (subheadings, bulleted lists, numbered list of steps) to guide them through a set of directions in a recipe.

▶ **Teaching Tips**

Before Reading
- Engage prior knowledge of recipes: what they are, who uses them, and how they convey information.
- Preview key terms: *sesame*, *benne* (BEH-nee), *ingredients*, *utensils*, *spatula*.
- Have students scan the page to notice that the recipe has four main parts: introduction, list of ingredients, list of utensils, and directions consisting of numbered steps.

During Reading
- Encourage students to highlight unfamiliar words or phrases for clarification.
- Suggest that students link the materials and utensils to the steps that use them.

After Reading
- If possible, have students make Benne Wafers in school or at home. (Check for possible food allergies ahead of time.) Ask students why it's important to read the entire set of instructions and ask any questions they may have before attempting to make a recipe.

Common Core Connections

RI.3.1, RI.3.2, RI.3.3, RI.3.4, RI.3.5, RI.3.7, RI.3.8, RI.3.10 • RF.3.3, RF.3.4 • W.3.10 • L.3.1, L.3.2, L.3.3, L.3.4, L.3.5, L.3.6

Complexity Index

Quantitative:
Lexile 590

Qualitative	1	2	3	4	5
Purpose			✳		
Structure			✳		
Language		✳			
Knowledge		✳			

Reader & Task

- Students who have never helped to prepare food "from scratch" may be unfamiliar with the typical format of a written recipe.
- Help students understand why the text is broken down into parts and sequential steps by asking how the outcome might change if the steps were not in order.

Passage 15 Place Names • page 54

Informational Text: Geography Article/Map

▶ **Focus** Students apply word-study, classifying, and inferencing skills to interpret geographical information from text and a related map.

▶ **Teaching Tips**

Before Reading
- Highlight Oregon and your state (if it is different) on a United States map. Invite students to compare and contrast the two states in every way they can.
- Use the question that precedes the passage to get students thinking about the origins of place names.

During Reading
- Have students stop after reading each section of the article to check their understanding. Encourage them to think through each place-name example to see why it fits its category.

After Reading
- Post a large map of your state (or a different state if you live in Oregon) for students to examine. Have groups search the map for examples of towns or bodies of water whose names fall into the categories of place names identified in this article.

Common Core Connections

RI.3.1, RI.3.2, RI.3.3, RI.3.4, RI.3.5, RI.3.7, RI.3.8, RI.3.10 • RF.3.3, RF.3.4 • W.3.10 • L.3.1, L.3.2, L.3.3, L.3.4, L.3.5, L.3.6

Complexity Index

Quantitative:
Lexile 610

Qualitative	1	2	3	4	5
Purpose			✳		
Structure				✳	
Language				✳	
Knowledge				✳	

Reader & Task

- Students may never have pondered the origin of place names.
- Reread lines 9–16 and encourage students to use the information in the text to predict how each place on the map got its name. Have them make a four-column chart (representing the four common ways) to organize their thinking.

25 Complex Text Passages to Meet the Common Core: Literature and Informational Texts, Grade 3 © 2014 by Scholastic Teaching Resources

Passage 16 — Bring Back Snacks • page 56

Informational Text: Persuasive Essay/Chart

▶ **Focus** Students read and analyze a well-constructed and effective persuasive essay.

▶ **Teaching Tips**

Before Reading
- Introduce *persuade* and the related form *persuasive*. Discuss what it means to attempt to persuade someone.
- Clarify the distinction between an argument as a battle of words and insults and an argument as a reasoned, organized plan of persuasion.

During Reading
- Encourage students to notice the boldface subheadings and how they help to clarify the writer's argument.
- Tell students to pause after each paragraph to identify its specific purpose in the overall argument the writer makes.
- Direct students' attention to the chart. Ask: *Why might the writer have included this information?*

After Reading
- Invite students to respond to the essay. Ask questions, such as: *Is it clear? Is it persuasive? Do you agree with the problem(s)? The proposed solution? What benefits would you expect? Would you add anything?*

Common Core Connections

RI.3.1, RI.3.2, RI.3.4, RI.3.5, RI.3.7, RI.3.8, RI.3.10 • RF.3.3, RF.3.4 • W.3.10 • L.3.1, L.3.2, L.3.3, L.3.4, L.3.5, L.3.6

Complexity Index

Quantitative: Lexile 660

Qualitative	1	2	3	4	5
Purpose			✳		
Structure		✳			
Language		✳			
Knowledge	✳				

Reader & Task

- Students may be very motivated by the issue but less familiar with a written argument.
- Be sensitive to the discomfort some students may feel who come from poverty or arrive at school not having eaten.
- Have students summarize the key parts of a persuasive essay, using this piece as a model.

Passage 17 — Endurance Sports • page 58

Informational Text: Sports Article

▶ **Focus** Students identify the characteristics and demands of endurance sports and use background information and direct quotations to understand one athlete's drive and motivation.

▶ **Teaching Tips**

Before Reading
- Preview the selection by having students read the title, the question that precedes the passage, the boldface subheadings, glossary box, and the photo.

During Reading
- Encourage students to use context clues to figure out the meanings of unfamiliar words.
- Guide students, as needed, on using the glossary box.

After Reading
- Invite students to design and make a poster that provides information about triathlons.

Common Core Connections

RI.3.1, RI.3.2, RI.3.3, RI.3.4, RI.3.5, RI.3.7, RI.3.8, RI.3.10 • RF.3.3, RF.3.4 • W.3.10 • L.3.1, L.3.2, L.3.3, L.3.4, L.3.5, L.3.6

Complexity Index

Quantitative: Lexile 680

Qualitative	1	2	3	4	5
Purpose				✳	
Structure			✳		
Language			✳		
Knowledge				✳	

Reader & Task

- Some students may have difficulty grasping the extraordinary effort, will, and discipline required to achieve success in endurance sports.
- Have students explain what is especially remarkable about Jason Lester's participation in endurance sports, and what this says about the kind of person Jason is.

Informational Text: Biographical Sketch

▶ **Focus** Using background information and direct quotations, this passage gives students insights into the life of a remarkable, multifaceted American.

▶ **Teaching Tips**

Before Reading
- Preview the various text elements of this piece: title, question that precedes the passage, body text, direct quotations in italics, sidebar with definitions, and photo with caption.

During Reading
- Encourage students to reread each quotation to ensure comprehension.
- Point out to students that direct quotations are usually shown within quotation marks; sometimes, however, especially if they are long, quotations can be italicized, and set off from the main part of the text, as they are in this piece.

After Reading
- Share with students the dictionary definition of the word *endeavor*. Discuss why this word is a fitting name for a spacecraft and an accurate description of Dr. Jemison.

Common Core Connections

RI.3.1, RI.3.2, RI.3.3, RI.3.4, RI.3.5, RI.3.7, RI.3.8, RI.3.10 • RF.3.3, RF.3.4 • W.3.10
• L.3.1, L.3.2, L.3.3, L.3.4, L.3.5, L.3.6

Complexity Index

Quantitative:
Lexile 700

Qualitative	1	2	3	4	5
Purpose			✳		
Structure					✳
Language			✳		
Knowledge			✳		

Reader & Task

- Students may be able to decode the quotations but find their meanings elusive.
- Have students identify evidence in the piece that show why Mae Jemison has become such a well-rounded person.

Informational Text: Social Studies Article/Annotated Photo

▶ **Focus** Students examine an annotated photo to identify and understand the many parts of a familiar object—a one-dollar bill.

▶ **Teaching Tips**

Before Reading
- Brainstorm with students to list what they recall about the face of a dollar bill.
- Preview challenging terms, such as *serial number*, *treasury*, and *seal*.

During Reading
- Encourage students to highlight unfamiliar words or phrases within each description.
- Discuss how the labeled captions accompanying the photo are useful for learning about this topic. (For example, *they provide detailed information about features on the bill and are an effective way of presenting information about the topic.*)

After Reading
- Extend by inviting students to find out about other features on the dollar bill not included in this piece. They might also compare and contrast the front and back of a one-dollar bill, or they can compare and contrast the features on the dollar bill with those on a five- or ten-dollar bill.

Common Core Connections

RI.3.1, RI.3.2, RI.3.4, RI.3.5, RI.3.7, RI.3.8, RI.3.10 • RF.3.3, RF.3.4 • W.3.10
• L.3.1, L.3.2, L.3.3, L.3.4, L.3.5, L.3.6

Complexity Index

Quantitative:
Lexile 710

Qualitative	1	2	3	4	5
Purpose			✳		
Structure					✳
Language				✳	
Knowledge			✳		

Reader & Task

- Some students may find the complexity of the visual presentation challenging.
- Have students describe some of the features in the design of a dollar bill that they never noticed before.

Passage 20 — A Prickly Idea • page 64

Informational Text: Science & Technology Article

▶ **Focus** Students make connections to understand the cause-and-effect origin of a now-common technology.

▶ **Teaching Tips**

Before Reading
- Discuss the meaning of and relationships between the terms *technology* (the use of science and engineering to do practical things) and *invention* (a new or creative idea for a process, product, or device).

During Reading
- Encourage students to look for clues within a sentence or paragraph to help unlock the meaning of unfamiliar words.

After Reading
- Help students use the images to understand the connection between burrs and Velcro. Clarify that Velcro has two parts that connect, while the burr has only the hooks and clings to something else (for example, fabric or animal fur) that serves as the loops.

Common Core Connections

RI.3.1, RI.3.2, RI.3.3, RI.3.4, RI.3.5, RI.3.7, RI.3.8, RI.3.10 • RF.3.3, RF.3.4 • W.3.10 • L.3.1, L.3.2, L.3.3, L.3.4, L.3.5, L.3.6

Complexity Index

Quantitative: Lexile 720

Qualitative	1	2	3	4	5
Purpose			✳		
Structure		✳			
Language		✳			
Knowledge			✳		

Reader & Task

- Students are likely to have interest in reading about the fascinating origin of a fastening product they know and use.
- Have students summarize the chain of events that led to the invention of Velcro.

Passage 21 — Make Sense • page 66

Informational Text: Language Arts Essay/Idioms

▶ **Focus** Students visualize, generalize, and extrapolate to find meaning in simple idioms.

▶ **Teaching Tips**

Before Reading
- Define *idiom* as a saying whose meaning is not the same as the meaning of its individual words. Give common examples, such as *a fish out of water* or *catch my eye*, and discuss.

During Reading
- Point out to students that each idiom appears in *italics*.
- Invite reading partners to discuss each of the essay's three sections to help them grasp the meaning of the given idiom.

After Reading
- Challenge students to write a real-life anecdote (real or fictional) that would feature one or more of the idioms examined in this essay.

Common Core Connections

RI.3.1, RI.3.2, RI.3.3, RI.3.4, RI.3.5, RI.3.7, RI.3.8, RI.3.10 • RF.3.3, RF.3.4 • W.3.10 • L.3.1, L.3.2, L.3.3, L.3.4, L.3.5, L.3.6

Complexity Index

Quantitative: Lexile 740

Qualitative	1	2	3	4	5
Purpose			✳		
Structure		✳			
Language		✳			
Knowledge		✳			

Reader & Task

- English Language Learners may have difficulty interpreting idioms, which are, by definition, not literal.
- Have students express in their own words what the three idioms in this essay mean.

Informational Text: Friendly Letter

▶ **Focus** Readers use text details in a friendly letter to visualize a setting and a personal experience.

▶ **Teaching Tips**

Before Reading
- Review the elements of a friendly letter: greeting (followed by a comma), body (main text), closing (also followed by a comma), and signature.
- Preview the passage by reading its title and the question that precedes the text, and by discussing the photo. Engage prior knowledge about hot-air balloons.

During Reading
- Correctly pronounce for students the terms for the instruments in line 19 as *al-TIM-uh-ter* and *vair-EE-OM-ih-ter*.
- Encourage students to reread sentences or paragraphs as needed to better understand concepts or descriptions presented.

After Reading
- Instruct students to generate questions they might pose to Clay, Todd, or Marcy about this adventure.

Common Core Connections

RI.3.1, RI.3.2, RI.3.3, RI.3.4, RI.3.5, RI.3.7, RI.3.8, RI.3.10 • RF.3.3, RF.3.4 • W.3.10 • L.3.1, L.3.2, L.3.3, L.3.4, L.3.5, L.3.6

Complexity Index

Quantitative: Lexile 750

Qualitative	1	2	3	4	5
Purpose			✳		
Structure		✳			
Language				✳	
Knowledge				✳	

Reader & Task

- Students may be able to decode the passage, but may not grasp the science concepts relating to balloon flight.
- Have students identify comparison statements Clay uses to accurately describe the balloon flight experience.

Informational Text: Historical Essay/Chart

▶ **Focus** Students integrate information from text, a chart, and an image to develop connections between foods of the past and the present.

▶ **Teaching Tips**

Before Reading
- Preview the three components of this passage: main text with boldface subheadings, a two-column chart, and an illustration with caption.

During Reading
- Instruct students to pause after each paragraph and recall its main points before going on.
- Encourage students to describe how the chart and the picture support and extend information in the main text.

After Reading
- Challenge students to write a one-paragraph summary of this essay.
- Extend by making a simple corn dish with students, such as johnnycakes or Indian pudding. (Check for possible food allergies ahead of time.)

Common Core Connections

RI.3.1, RI.3.2, RI.3.3, RI.3.4, RI.3.5, RI.3.7, RI.3.8, RI.3.10 • RF.3.3, RF.3.4 • W.3.10 • L.3.1, L.3.2, L.3.3, L.3.4, L.3.5, L.3.6

Complexity Index

Quantitative: Lexile 770

Qualitative	1	2	3	4	5
Purpose				✳	
Structure				✳	
Language			✳		
Knowledge			✳		

Reader & Task

- Some students may not know that food itself has a history and development. Many will be surprised at the various and diverse uses for corn.
- Have students explain the notion that food can have a history. Have them support their response with details from the essay.

Informational Text: Life Science Article/Annotated Diagram

▶ **Focus** Students examine an annotated diagram to identify and understand the body parts of a marine mammal.

▶ **Teaching Tips**

Before Reading
- Brainstorm with students to list questions they may have about whales.

During Reading
- Have students list questions that arise as they read about whales.
- Discuss how the labeled and captioned diagram is an effective text feature for learning about this topic. (For example, *it provides more information and shows where the body parts are and what they do.*)

After Reading
- Revisit the questions students posed before reading to see which, if any, have been addressed.
- To review, invite students to generate and write down new questions based on facts they learned from this selection. Collect, shuffle, and redistribute for classmates to answer.

Common Core Connections

RI.3.1, RI.3.2, RI.3.3, RI.3.4, RI.3.5, RI.3.7, RI.3.8, RI.3.10 • RF.3.3, RF.3.4 • W.3.10 • L.3.1, L.3.2, L.3.3, L.3.4, L.3.5, L.3.6

Complexity Index

Quantitative: Lexile 780

Qualitative	1	2	3	4	5
Purpose			❋		
Structure				❋	
Language			❋		
Knowledge			❋		

Reader & Task

- Some students may find it challenging to navigate the information presented on the diagram.
- Name a body part mentioned in the diagram. Ask students to describe its location on a whale and tell something special about it. Repeat for all parts mentioned.

Informational Text: Historical Anecdote

▶ **Focus** Students understand an historical decision from an opposing point of view.

▶ **Teaching Tips**

Before Reading
- Explain to students that an anecdote is a short, amusing, or interesting story, often part of a biography or history.
- Introduce the term *symbol* as an object or image that stands for something else. Symbols can be concrete (for example, a sign showing a red line through a car means no parking allowed) or abstract (a red cross stands for a hospital or ambulance). Brainstorm familiar symbols students encounter every day.

During Reading
- Encourage students to mark words or phrases that are unfamiliar to them, or jot down questions in the margins for later discussion.

After Reading
- Tell students that Benjamin Franklin expressed his views on the National Bird in a letter he wrote to his daughter Sally in 1784. Challenge students to use details from the anecdote to create the letter Franklin might have written.

Common Core Connections

RI.3.1, RI.3.2, RI.3.3, RI.3.4, RI.3.5, RI.3.6, RI.3.7, RI.3.8, RI.3.10 • RF.3.3, RF.3.4 • W.3.10 • L.3.1, L.3.2, L.3.3, L.3.4, L.3.5, L.3.6

Complexity Index

Quantitative: Lexile 790

Qualitative	1	2	3	4	5
Purpose				❋	
Structure		❋			
Language				❋	
Knowledge				❋	

Reader & Task

- Some students may lack adequate prior knowledge of basic American history and the power of national symbols.
- As students read and study the photos, have them fill in a T-chart that compares an eagle with a turkey.

Name _____ Date _____

Kadimba's Field
Bantu Folktale

How does Kadimba use his cleverness to avoid work?

1 Clever Kadimba was a lazy hare. It was time to plant crops
2 to feed his family, but he hated work. Tangled bushes throughout
3 his field made the job daunting. Even after clearing the field,
4 Kadimba would still have to dig rows for his crops.
5   Kadimba hatched a plan. He dragged a thick rope across
6 his field. Then he waited by one end for Elephant to appear.
7 Kadimba dared Elephant to a tug-of-war. The tusker roared
8 but agreed. He twisted his trunk around the rope. Kadimba
9 said, "When you feel my pull, then pull back." He raced to the
10 opposite side of the tangled field and rested by the other end of
11 the rope. Elephant waited patiently.
12   Soon Hippo waddled by. Kadimba offered this giant the same
13 challenge. Hippo agreed, letting the hare wrap the rope 'round
14 his muddy body. Kadimba said, "When you feel my pull, then
15 pull back." Hippo waited good-naturedly.
16   Kadimba then dashed to the middle of the rope and tugged
17 in each direction. Feeling the pull, Elephant and Hippo began
18 tugging. They yanked,
19 grunted, and heaved
20 in astonishment. They
21 pulled back and forth,
22 left and right, struggling
23 until nightfall. By then,
24 the rope had torn out all
25 the tangled bushes; the
26 thrashing had softened the
27 soil. Kadimba's field was
28 ready for planting.

Name _____ Date _____ **27**

Kadimba's Field

▶ **Answer each question. Give evidence from the folktale.**

1 The *daunting* job (line 3) made Kadimba feel _____ .

○ A. heartbroken   ○ B. discouraged   ○ C. sleepy   ○ D. proud

How did you choose your answer? _____

_____

2 Which type of character is Kadimba?

○ A. a brave hero   ○ C. a sneaky trickster

○ B. an angry loser   ○ D. an innocent victim

What in the text helped you answer? _____

_____

_____

3 Why did Hippo and Elephant feel so astonished (lines 19 and 20)? _____

_____

_____

4 Why did Kadimba rest for a while (lines 9–11)? _____

_____

5 Explain Kadimba's clever plan. _____

_____

_____

_____

_____

Name _____ Date _____

Follow Me

What makes this story an adventure?

1   "When this volcano blew about a thousand years ago,
2   it sent the local inhabitants scurrying to safety," Mimi
3   reported as we neared our destination.
4   We drove through a moonlike landscape, where plants
5   and trees struggled to grow. Then I saw Sunset Crater. It
6   was a huge black cone with tinges of orange and yellow.
7   It was magnificent! We parked the car and began to walk
8   the winding trail along its base. "I've got the flashlights,"
9   Mimi said.
10   *Flashlights?* I wondered.
11   I soon found out the
12 reason for them when she
13 stopped and pointed to a
14 narrow, dark opening. "Follow
15 me," she called. "We're about
16 to enter a tunnel made by
17 lava. Zip up your sweatshirt."

18   We scrambled down into
19 darkness. It got cold very
20 quickly as we descended; it
21 got scary, too. We clambered
22 over sharp and slippery rocks and had to duck under
23 hanging rocks that looked like icicles. The ceiling was so
24 low in parts that we had to crawl. Soon the walls began to
25 close in on us. At that point we stopped, took in the eerie
26 silence, and then made our way out.
27   "Amazing lava tube, right?" Mimi asked, once we were
28 safely above ground.
29   "Awesome!" I answered, relieved to see blue sky.

Name _____ Date _____   29

Follow Me

▶ **Answer each question. Give evidence from the adventure.**

1 If you *descended* (line 20), you _____ .

    ○ A. climbed up   ○ B. went down   ○ C. wondered   ○ D. explored

    How did you choose your answer? _____

    _____

2 Which sentence best describes a *lava tube* (line 27)?

    ○ A. It is a tunnel made by lava.   ○ C. It is a kind of volcano.

    ○ B. It is a moonlike landscape.   ○ D. It is a winding trail.

    What in the text helped you answer? _____

    _____

    _____

3 Why did Mimi bring along flashlights? _____

    _____

    _____

4 What would be scary about going into a lava tube for the first time? Explain.

    _____

    _____

5 Explain what "the walls began to close in on us" (lines 24 and 25) means.

    _____

    _____

    _____

Name _____ Date _____

A "Punny" Pair

What elements link these two jokes?

1 King Alfred's castle was under
2 siege from a powerful enemy. The
3 knights were low on food, so the
4 king had to send someone for
5 help. But by now all the king's
6 horses had been lost in battle.
7 "We must find a way to get help,"
8 commanded the king.
9   "Yes, Sire, but we have no more
10 horses," replied the head knight.
11 "I fear that even our fastest knight
12 will be captured or killed if he goes
13 out on foot."
14   "Is there no other animal
15 fit to ride?" demanded King Alfred. "What about my mighty
16 wolfhound Fritz? Surely he could carry any rider."
17   "Sire!" argued the leader. "Fritz is far too nasty. Look at his
18 snarling fangs. *I wouldn't send a knight out on a dog like this!*"

19   Miles and Giles were talking. Miles
20 said, "A duck, a frog, and a skunk went
21 to the movies every Saturday. Today
22 they hoped to see the latest comedy
23 film. Tickets cost one dollar each. Why
24 was the skunk the only one who could
25 NOT afford a ticket?"
26   Giles replied, "I know! The duck
27 had a *bill*, the frog had a *greenback*,
28 but the skunk had only a *scent*."

25 Complex Text Passages to Meet the Common Core: Literature and Informational Texts, Grade 3 © 2014 by Scholastic Teaching Resources

Name _____ Date _____

A "Punny" Pair

▶ **Answer each question. Give evidence from the jokes.**

1 When a castle is *under siege* (lines 1 and 2), the people inside _____.

  ○ A. cannot see   ○ C. have no leader

  ○ B. cannot defend themselves   ○ D. have no animals

How did you choose your answer? _____

_____

2 Which best describes a *greenback* (line 27)? _____

  ○ A. an intelligent kind of frog   ○ C. a nickname for a U.S. dollar bill

  ○ B. a type of American soldier   ○ D. a fruit or vegetable that isn't ripe yet

What in the text helped you answer? _____

_____

3 Summarize King Alfred's problem. _____

_____

_____

_____

4 How can you tell that the story about Miles and Giles is a joke? _____

_____

_____

5 What do the two funny jokes have in common? _____

_____

_____

Name _____ Date _____

One Clever Cat

What can you tell about Tiger from her actions and reactions?

1   Inez opened her door, and Lupe walked in. Tiger, Inez's
2 cuddly cat who had been dozing on the couch, looked up
3 in fear.
4   "Oh, Tiger, I could hug you forever!" Lupe scooped up
5 the jittery cat and wrapped her arms around her.
6   Tiger wriggled out of her grasp and sped away. But
7 Lupe, even dressed up as she was, was quick enough to
8 grab hold of her again. Lupe then settled onto the couch,
9 Tiger squirming on her lap.
10   Fidgeting just enough to escape again, Tiger leapt to
11 the floor and raced behind a chair across the room.
12   "Forget the cat, Lupe," Inez said, as her cousin started
13 in pursuit. "Come with me and choose a necklace."
14   When the two returned, Tiger was nowhere in sight.
15 Lupe began poking under and around the furniture.
16   "Never mind that," Inez replied. "Go or you'll be late.
17 I'll say goodbye for you."
18   "Tiger, where are you?" she
19 called after Lupe was gone. A
20 meek meow drew her attention
21 to the kitchen. There was Tiger,
22 peeking out from a cabinet above
23 the refrigerator. The wily cat came
24 down from her perch and scampered
25 toward Inez, purring happily.

26   "Oh, you smart kitten," Inez said
27 with a knowing smile. "Your secret is
28 safe with me."

Name _____ Date _____

One Clever Cat

▶ **Answer each question. Give evidence from the story.**

1 A cat that acts *jittery* (line 5) most likely feels _____.

○ A. happy   ○ B. lonely   ○ C. hungry   ○ D. nervous

How did you pick your answer? _____

_____

_____

2 Why did Lupe stop by Inez's house?

○ A. Lupe hoped to play with Tiger.   ○ C. Lupe needed help with her homework.

○ B. Lupe wished to borrow some jewelry.   ○ D. Lupe wanted to see Inez's furniture.

What in the story helped you answer? _____

_____

3 Explain how the title fits this story. _____

_____

_____

4 Why was Tiger purring happily at the end of the story? _____

_____

_____

5 Explain why Inez had *a knowing smile* (line 27). _____

_____

_____

Name _____ Date _____

Fishing on the Rogue
Tall Tale From Oregon

What features make this story a tall tale?

1   That there is Dunkelberger gravel bar. It's one of the finest
2   fishing spots on the Rogue River. In boats you can fish most
3   anywhere. But if you're stuck on the bank—or if you prefer solid
4   ground—then this place is for you.
5   Our Rogue River is famous for steelhead. Fishing's one of the
6   few fun things to do around these parts in our rainy season. It's
7   so darn tiresome staying indoors. So we locals came up with ways
8   around it.
9   We steelhead lovers weld rod holders to the bumpers of our
10   trucks. Look! There's one over yonder! Folks drive out to the end of
11   Dunkelberger gravel bar, throw out a hook and line, return to the
12   truck, and roll up the windows. We set there, warm and dry, until
13   we snag a steelhead. And it usually doesn't take long.
14   My wife Mabel was here just last week. She hauled in a big
15   steelhead. When she saw the rod bend, she knew she had a bite.
16   So she put the truck in reverse and stomped on the gas. Mabel
17   yanked that fish thirty feet up the bank, driving backwards.
18   We sure know how to fish in an Oregon winter!

Name _____ Date _____

Fishing on the Rogue

▶ **Answer each question. Give evidence from the tall tale.**

1 A *steelhead* (line 5) is

   ○ A. part of a river.   ○ C. a type of fish.

   ○ B. part of a truck.   ○ D. a winter sport.

How did you choose your answer? _____

_____

2 Which best explains why Rogue River fishing is done from a truck?

   ○ A. You sit up high and can see better from a truck.

   ○ B. You need a truck to carry so much fishing gear.

   ○ C. You can stay out of the rain if you fish from a truck.

   ○ D. There are no safe spots to stand by the river.

What in the text helped you answer? _____

_____

3 Based on this tall tale, when is the rainy season in Oregon? _____

_____

4 Describe a gravel bar. Use the photo to help you. _____

_____

5 What about this story makes it a tall tale? _____

_____

_____

_____

Name _____ Date _____

The Crow and the Pitcher
Based on a Fable by Aesop

What is the crow's problem, and how does she solve it?

1   One hot day, a crow
2   was feverish from thirst.
3   She came upon a clay
4   pitcher that had once been
5   full of water. But now the
6   pitcher was nearly empty.
7   The parched crow tried to
8   reach the water with her
9   sharp beak, but the neck of
10 the pitcher was too narrow.
11 Again and again she tried,
12 but the pitcher was too tall
13 and the water too shallow
14 for her beak to reach even
15 one tiny drop.
16   Nearly desperate, the
17 crow stopped to think. Soon an idea came—she could make the
18 water rise! She grabbed a pebble and dropped it into the pitcher.
19 Then she took another pebble and dropped it in. Then she let fall
20 into the pitcher another pebble. One pebble at a time, the crow
21 kept at her plan. Each pebble made the water level rise a bit. And
22 each rise spurred the crow to continue.
23   At long last, the water level was high enough for the crow to
24 satisfy her thirst. And so she lived to see another day.

25   **MORAL:** Little by little does the trick.

Name _____ Date _____

The Crow and the Pitcher

▶ **Answer each question. Give evidence from the fable.**

1 If you feel *parched* (line 7), you would probably want _____.

○ A. something to eat   ○ C. something to drink

○ B. somewhere to sit   ○ D. someone to play with

How did you pick your answer? _____

_____

2 Which part of the pitcher is the *neck* (line 9)?

○ A. its base   ○ B. its height   ○ C. its handle   ○ D. its thinnest part

What in the text helped you answer? _____

_____

3 Explain the crow's problem. _____

_____

_____

4 How do the pebbles make the water rise? _____

_____

_____

5 Explain the meaning of the moral in your own words. _____

_____

_____

_____

Name _____ Date _____

Norse All-Father
Nordic Myth

How would you compare and contrast Odin with other mythical gods?

1   Odin was the most powerful Norse god. As lord of the sky,
2   Odin guided souls to the afterlife. He ruled the present time of
3   all things. He could predict the future of all humankind. And he
4   could gaze into the past.
5   Odin ruled from his throne, built in the highest tower
6   of his silver palace in Asgard. From that grand seat, Odin
7   could observe all of heaven and earth. Two black ravens sat
8   beside him. Their names were Hugin (meaning *thought*) and
9   Munin (meaning *memory*). Each day, Odin sent his ravens to
10 gather information from the whole world. Upon their return,
11 they reported what they saw and heard. Their thoughts and
12 memories became Odin's own.
13   Odin was mighty. With a single
14 word, he could smother fire, calm
15 waves, or redirect the wind. He
16 could visit far-off lands in his mind
17 or through the memories of others.
18 Odin knew the location of all the
19 world's treasures. And he could shift
20 into any shape he wanted or needed.
21   Odin prized wisdom and beauty.
22 His voice was so soft that those he
23 spoke to believed they were hearing
24 pure truth. Odin was deeply skillful
25 in gaining knowledge, guarding it,
26 and using it to his advantage.

Name _____ Date _____

Norse All-Father

▶ **Answer each question. Give evidence from the myth.**

1 What was Asgard (line 6)?

○ A. Odin's home   ○ B. Odin's son   ○ C. Odin's raven   ○ D. Odin's throne

How did you choose your answer? _____

_____

2 Which does NOT describe Odin?

○ A. He was the most powerful.   ○ C. He could make fire.

○ B. He valued knowledge.   ○ D. He could predict the future.

What in the text helped you answer? _____

_____

_____

3 What was special about Odin's voice? _____

_____

_____

4 Give two synonyms for the word *gaze* (line 4). _____

_____

5 An old saying states that "Knowledge is power." What about Odin shows that he would agree with that saying?

_____

_____

Name _____   Date _____

The Mirror Stirs

What frightened the twins?

1   After a long ride on a
2   bumpy dirt road, the Motts
3   arrived at Prickly Pear, a
4   ghost town. A few lonely
5   old buildings and parts
6   of buildings stood quietly
7   in the broiling midday
8   sun. Mom parked the car
9   between the skeleton that
10 had been a schoolhouse
11 and the remains of a small
12 adobe jail. It was really,
13 really hot.

14 While Dad was getting out his camera to take photos,
15 the twins asked if they could explore the jail. Permission
16 granted, Tom and Ann raced into the dilapidated old
17 structure.
18   It was dark inside, but surprisingly cool. After a moment
19 something grabbed their attention in the dim light—their
20 reflections! At first taken aback, they realized that they were
21 seeing what remained of a framed, cracked mirror. They
22 each let out a sigh of relief. But then, the mirror began to
23 wriggle a little. And then, suddenly, it lurched toward them!
24   They ran like jackrabbits from that spooky jail! Both
25 were panting and sweaty when they reached their parents,
26 who were talking to a man sitting in a truck. They had to
27 hold their tongues.
28   "Howdy, folks. Anybody spot my dog, Wyatt?" the man
29 asked. "He jumped from my pick-up. That usually means
30 he's looking for a cool, private place to hunker down."

Name _____ Date _____

The Mirror Stirs

▶ **Answer each question. Give evidence from the mystery.**

1 A structure that is *dilapidated* (line 16) would be _____.

○ A. cool and dark   ○ C. made of adobe

○ B. broken down   ○ D. filled with ghosts

How did you choose your answer? _____

_____

2 Which best describes a *ghost town* (line 4)?

○ A. It is a cemetery.

○ B. It is home to skeletons and ghosts.

○ C. It is a town that gets broiled by the sun.

○ D. It is a town that nobody lives in anymore.

What evidence in the text helped you answer? _____

_____

3 What does it mean that the twins *ran like jackrabbits* (line 24)? _____

_____

4 Why did the mirror move? _____

_____

5 What does the author mean by comparing the schoolhouse to a *skeleton* (lines 9 and 10)?

_____

_____

Name _____ Date _____

A New House

What clues tell you that this story is set in the past?

1   Pa stopped the wagon when we reached our land. But there
2 was no home in sight, only flat prairie. "We'll build our house
3 here," he said, wiping his brow.
4   "How?" I asked, since I saw not one tree.
5   "We'll use the sod beneath our feet, Jenny," he answered.
6 "This buffalo grass has dense roots perfect for holding the soil."
7   Pa and Silas set up a simple lean-to for shelter during
8 construction. Then they went into town to get boards, pegs, and
9 a grasshopper plow. Meanwhile, Ma and I set to cooking and
10 making our lean-to livable.
11 When the menfolk got back,
12 we all ate and went to sleep,
13 exhausted.

14   At first light, Pa and Silas set
15 to work. Pa plowed long strips of
16 sod a foot wide and four inches
17 thick. Silas came behind with
18 a spade to cut each sod strip
19 into 3-foot long bricks. It was
20 difficult, dirty work.

Gathering sod bricks

21   After all the sod was cut, Pa
22 and Silas began making walls,
23 grass-side down, two feet thick.
24 Pa left room to set wooden
25 frames for a door and window,
26 and Silas drove wooden pegs
27 into the sod to hold the frames
28 in place. They spent the whole
29 day and there was still much to
30 be done.

Building a house with sod bricks

25 Complex Text Passages to Meet the Common Core: Literature and Informational Texts, Grade 3 © 2014 by Scholastic Teaching Resources

Name _____ Date _____

A New House

▶ **Answer each question. Give evidence from the story.**

1 Who is telling the story?

○ A. Jenny   ○ B. Silas   ○ C. Ma   ○ D. Pa

How did you choose your answer? _____

_____

2 Why did Pa and Silas go into town (line 8)?

○ A. They needed food and firewood.   ○ C. They needed to go to a bank.

○ B. They needed building supplies.   ○ D. They wanted to buy land.

What in the text helped you answer? _____

_____

_____

3 Describe what *sod* is (line 5). _____

_____

4 Describe the walls of the new house. Use details from the text. _____

_____

_____

5 What is a *lean-to*? Why would the family build one before building the house?

_____

_____

_____

Name _____ Date _____

Gary's Tuba

What is the interviewer's most important job?

1   My neighbor Gary plays the tuba. I spoke with Gary to learn
2   more about his instrument.

3   **Me:** *Gary, let's start with facts about your tuba.*

4   **Gary:** My tuba is made of brass, a golden metal mixture.
5   My tuba weighs about 30 pounds. If I could unroll it,
6   it would stretch out about 16 feet!

7   **Me:** *Is a tuba the biggest instrument an orchestra has?*

8   **Gary:** No, but it plays the lowest notes. It is the
9   biggest instrument in the brass family.

10   **Me:** *How does the tuba make sound?*

11   **Gary:** I blow air and buzz my lips together on
12   the mouthpiece. The air vibrates and gets
13   louder because the tuba is like an echo chamber.
14   You hear sound as it comes out the opening we
15   call the *bell.*

16   **Me:** *How do you get all that air?*

17   **Gary:** I suck in air like a living vacuum cleaner!
18   I take many huge breaths to keep the sound going.

19   **Me:** *What do your hands do?*

20   **Gary:** My right hand presses the *valves* to change
21   notes. My left hand helps me adjust notes with
22   *slides.* Or it can just rest.

23   **Me:** *Do tuba notes hurt your ears?*

24   **Gary:** Not at all! The sound is warm and mellow.

25   **Me:** *Can anybody learn to play the tuba?*

26   **Gary:** The more, the merrier! But most kids start in
27   middle school.

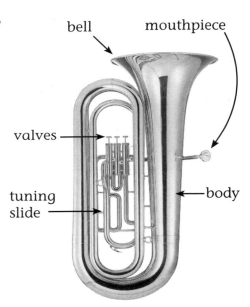

bell   mouthpiece

valves

tuning
slide

body

Famous Tuba Tunes

- "Tubby the Tuba"
- Jabba the Hutt Theme
  From *Return of the Jedi*
- Voice of Alien Ship in
  *Close Encounters of the
  Third Kind*

Name _____ Date _____

Gary's Tuba

▶ **Answer each question. Give evidence from the interview and diagram.**

1 Which family does the tuba belong to?

  ○ A. the instrument family   ○ C. the brass family

  ○ B. the orchestra family   ○ D. the echo family

What in the text helped you answer? _____

_____

2 Based on information in the interview, which is NOT true about the tuba?

  ○ A. Anyone can learn to play it.

  ○ B. It is the largest instrument in the orchestra.

  ○ C. It has valves and slides to change and adjust notes.

  ○ D. It plays the lowest notes in the orchestra.

What in the text helped you answer? _____

_____

3 Look at the diagram. Find the place on the tuba where the sound comes out. Do you think that its name makes sense? Explain.

_____

4 Why would Gary suggest that kids wait until middle school to take tuba lessons?

_____

_____

5 Why does the interviewer ask Gary if tuba notes hurt his ears (line 23)?

_____

_____

Name _____ Date _____

Wash and Dry

What features make the directions on this sign easy to follow?

1 Welcome to *Lucy's Do-It-Yourself Laundry*! Wash and dry your
2 things in our clean and modern facility. All it takes are some quarters,
3 laundry soap, and your dirty clothes. Follow these simple steps.

4 **WASH**

5 **1.** Sort laundry by color. Put whites and lights into
6 one load, and darks into another load.
7 **2.** Open the washing machines and put in your
8 dirty items.
9 **3.** Add soap to each machine. Don't use too much!
10 **4.** Select the correct temperature setting for each
11 load. Choose hot or warm for whites and lights.
12 Choose cold for dark colors or delicate items.
13 **5.** Shut the door tightly. Insert quarters into the coin slot.
14 **6.** Press START. A complete cycle takes about 30 minutes.
15 **7.** When the washer stops, remove ALL items from the
16 machine.

17 **DRY**

18 **1.** Put items in the dryer. Add fabric softener sheets,
19 if you wish.
20 **2.** Select the correct temperature setting for each load.
21 Consider the size of the load and the types of fabrics
22 it includes.
23 **3.** Shut the door tightly. Insert quarters into the
24 coin slot. Press START.
25 **4.** When the dryer stops, remove ALL items from the
26 machine. Or, add more quarters as needed for
27 additional drying time.

Price List

Wash
$1.25 per load

Dry
25¢ for 10 min.

Name _____ Date _____

Wash and Dry

▶ **Answer each question. Give evidence from the sign.**

1 Where is this sign on display?

　○ A. in a school　　　　　○ C. in a hospital

　○ B. in a clothing store　　○ D. in a coin laundry

What in the text helped you answer? _____

_____

2 You are doing a load of wash. Which of these steps would you do first?

　○ A. Add the soap where it belongs.　　○ C. Press the START button.

　○ B. Put items into the machine.　　　○ D. Shut the door tightly.

What in the text helped you answer? _____

_____

3 About how long does it take a machine to wash one load of clothes? _____

_____

4 Mr. Hwang washes one load of laundry. Then he dries the load for 30 minutes. How much money does this cost in all? Explain.

_____

_____

5 Why are there more steps for WASH than for DRY? Explain. _____

_____

_____

_____

Name _____ Date _____

Hello, Roy G. Biv!

What helps you understand the meaning of the title of this article?

1　　Dorothy in *The Wizard of Oz* longed
2　to be "over the rainbow." The perfect
3　place she imagined wasn't real. But
4　rainbows are.
5　　A rainbow is a colorful arc in the
6　sky. You might see one when the sun
7　comes out after it rains. You also might
8　see one in the mist from a hose. You can
9　*see* rainbows but you can't *touch* them.
10　Rainbows don't take up space. So what
11　makes them real?
12　　The great scientist Sir Isaac Newton discovered important
13　ideas about light 450 years ago. He observed light to
14　determine how it moved. Newton figured out that light is
15　made of fast-moving bits of energy. Light can move through
16　air. It also moves through water and other materials.
17　　One day, Newton used an object called a *prism* to look at
18　light. A prism is a wedge-
19　shaped piece of clear glass.
20　When he held his prism up
21　to the sun, its visible (white)
22　light passed through the
23　glass. It came out the other
24　side. But the light was no
25　longer white. The prism
26　*refracted*, or bent, the white
27　light. It broke the light
28　apart into colors called
29　the *spectrum*. These are the
30　same colors you see in a
31　rainbow.

Do you know ROY G. BIV?

He's not a person. Roy G. Biv
is a memory shortcut. Each
letter in the "name" means a
color of the spectrum in order:
Red, **O**range, **Y**ellow, **G**reen,
Blue, **I**ndigo, and **V**iolet.

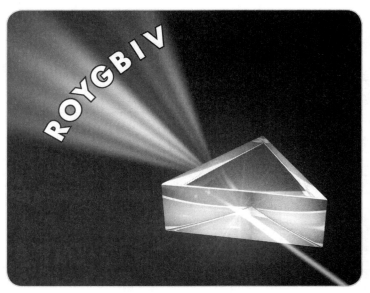

Name _____ Date _____

Hello, Roy G. Biv!

▶ **Answer each question. Give evidence from the article.**

1 What is NOT true about a rainbow?

○ A. It is shaped like an arc.   ○ C. You can see it in the sky.

○ B. You can grab hold of it.   ○ D. Its colors appear in the same order.

What in the text helped you answer? _____

_____

_____

2 Which of the following means the same as *refracted* (line 26)?

○ A. bent   ○ B. visible   ○ C. touched   ○ D. energetic

What in the text helped you answer? _____

_____

3 Who is Roy G. Biv? Explain. _____

_____

_____

4 Why does the author include Sir Isaac Newton in this article? _____

_____

_____

5 Why did the author begin the article with Dorothy from *The Wizard of Oz*?

_____

_____

Name _____ Date _____

Multiple Meanings

How can you sort through the many meanings of a word?

1 Imagine you are reading an exciting mystery. The main
2 character is in danger, and you can't wait to know what will
3 happen. Then you read a sentence, but the meaning of a simple
4 word just doesn't fit.

5 "Meet me in the rhubarb **plot** at midnight."

6 The *dictionary* can help you make sense of this word in the way
7 the author means it. It gives one or more meanings for every
8 word it lists. Look up the word *plot*. Find the meaning that works
9 best in the story.

How to say the word

10 Entry word   **plot** (plot)

11 **1.** NOUN a secret plan, especially for doing
12 something bad: *They hatched a plot to rob*
13 *the train.*

14 **2.** VERB to plan secretly with others to do
15 something wrong: *The princes plot against*
16 *the old king.*

17 **3.** NOUN the main story of a play, book,
18 movie, or poem: *The plot of this film involves*
19 *time travel.*

20 **4.** NOUN a small piece of land: *She tends her*
21 *tiny garden plot.*

22 **5.** VERB to make a map or diagram: *The*
23 *captain plots the ship's course.*

24 **6.** VERB in math, to locate or graph an exact
25 point: *Now plot (3, 4) on the coordinate grid.*

Definitions
with part
of speech

25 Complex Text Passages to Meet the Common Core: Literature and Informational Texts, Grade 3 © 2014 by Scholastic Teaching Resources

Name _____ Date _____

Multiple Meanings

▶ **Answer each question. Give evidence from the dictionary entry.**

1 How many different meanings of *plot* does this dictionary entry give?

○ A. one ○ B. two ○ C. five ○ D. six

How did the text help you answer? _____

_____

2 What does this dictionary entry NOT give?

○ A. other words that mean the same as *plot*

○ B. examples of sentences with *plot* in them

○ C. how to pronounce *plot*

○ D. the part of speech for each meaning of *plot*

How did you choose your answer? _____

_____

3 Which meaning of *plot* fits the sentence in line 5? Explain. _____

_____

_____

4 Explain what an *entry word* is (line 10)._____

_____

5 Read this sentence: Let's *plot* our trip to the beach.
Which meaning of *plot* best fits this sentence? Explain.

_____

_____

Name _____ Date _____

Healthy and Crispy

Why are only the directions given in number order?

1　　　Sesame seeds are very healthy to eat. They supply fiber,
2　protein, and vitamins. Best of all, they are available all over the
3　world. The Bantu people of Africa call sesame seeds *benne*. Make
4　these simple benne wafers for a sweet and tasty treat.

5　**Benne Wafers**　　Makes 24 thin wafers

6　**Ingredients**　　　　　　　　　　　**Utensils**

7　cooking spray　　　　　　　　　　● cookie sheets

8　$\frac{1}{2}$ cup sesame seeds　　　　　　　● measuring spoons and cups

9　6 tablespoons unsalted butter, soft　● frying pan

10　1 cup brown sugar, packed　　　　● mixing bowl, fork, and spoon

11　1 beaten egg　　　　　　　　　　● spatula

12　$\frac{1}{2}$ cup flour　　　　　　　　　　● cooling rack

13　$\frac{1}{4}$ teaspoon salt

14　$\frac{1}{2}$ teaspoon baking powder

15　1 teaspoon vanilla extract

16　**Directions**

17　**1.** Preheat oven to 350°F. Spray cookie sheets with cooking spray.

18　**2.** Gently toast sesame seeds in a dry frying pan. Stir until they turn
19　　　golden. Don't let them scorch.

20　**3.** Blend butter and brown sugar together in a bowl. Add egg, flour,
21　　　salt, baking powder, and vanilla. Combine until smooth.

22　**4.** Add toasted sesame seeds. Mix well.

23　**5.** Drop spoonfuls of dough onto cookie sheets. Allow room between
24　　　wafers because they spread as they bake.

25　**6.** Bake 12–13 minutes, or until the wafers turn golden brown.
26　　　Wait a few minutes. Then transfer them to a rack to cool. ENJOY!!!

25 Complex Text Passages to Meet the Common Core: Literature and Informational Texts, Grade 3 © 2014 by Scholastic Teaching Resources

Name _____ Date _____

Healthy and Crispy

▶ **Answer each question. Give evidence from the recipe.**

1 Which of the following is NOT true about sesame seeds?

  ○ A. They are healthy to eat.   ○ C. They supply fiber and vitamins.

  ○ B. They are available everywhere.   ○ D. They were discovered in Africa.

What in the text helped you answer? _____

_____

2 If you *scorch* (line 19) the sesame seeds, they will _____,

  ○ A. turn dark brown   ○ B. taste better   ○ C. feel cold   ○ D. spread

What in the text helped you answer? _____

_____

_____

3 Why are the Directions numbered, but not the Ingredients or Utensils? _____

_____

_____

4 Why do the directions appear *last* in the recipe? _____

_____

_____

5 What about the ingredients, utensils, and directions tell you that *wafers* (line 4) are a kind of cookie?

_____

_____

Name _____ Date _____

Place Names

How do places get their names?

1 In 1845, settlers Asa Lovejoy and Francis Pettygrove put down
2 roots beside a river in Oregon. Lovejoy came from Massachusetts.
3 He wanted to name the settlement *Boston*. Pettygrove, from
4 Maine, wanted to name it after his state's capital, *Portland*. They
5 flipped a penny and Pettygrove won. And that's how Oregon's
6 largest city got its name!
7 Towns and cities get named for different reasons. Here are
8 four common ones.

9 • After **other places**
10   Rome, New York, or New London, Connecticut
11 • After **geographical features**
12   Lakeland, Florida, or Pinetop, Arizona
13 • After **a famous person or early settler**
14   Lincoln, Nebraska, or Carson City, Nevada
15 • After **discoveries or events that took place there**
16   Dinosaur, Colorado, or Silver City, New Mexico

17 This map of Oregon shows
18 some of its towns and cities.
19 Think about how these places
20 may have gotten their names.

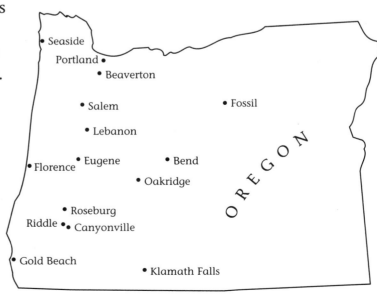

• Seaside
Portland •
    • Beaverton
• Salem   • Fossil
    • Lebanon
•Florence • Eugene   • Bend
                    • Oakridge
        • Roseburg
Riddle • • Canyonville
• Gold Beach
            • Klamath Falls

OREGON

Name _____ Date _____

Place Names

▶ **Answer each question. Give evidence from the article.**

1 Which sounds like the best reason for how Fossil, Oregon, got its name?

    ○ A. It was named for another place.

    ○ B. It was named for a geographical feature.

    ○ C. It was named for a discovery that took place there.

    ○ D. It was named for an early settler or famous person.

What in the text helped you answer? _____

_____

2 Which of the following towns on the map was most likely named for an early settler or famous person?

    ○ A. Canyonville   ○ B. Bend   ○ C. Eugene   ○ D. Riddle

What helped you answer? _____

_____

3 What connects Asa Lovejoy and Francis Pettygrove? _____

_____

4 Look at the map. List the names of three places that were probably named for a geographical feature.

_____

_____

5 Grants Pass is another place in Oregon. Suggest a sensible reason for its name.

_____

_____

Name _____ Date _____

Bring Back Snacks

How does the writer attempt to get readers to agree?

1 **The Problem** We kids get hungry. Whether we've eaten
2 a hearty breakfast, skipped our morning meal altogether,
3 or quickly wolfed down some toast while racing to school,
4 by late morning we are famished. We're focusing on our
5 bellies rather than on our schoolwork. We need to have a
6 daily morning snack time.

7   In kindergarten and first grade, we had snack time
8 every morning. We all looked forward to it. Even in
9 second grade, snack time was something we eagerly
10 awaited. Now, in third grade, snack time is gone. But our
11 hunger is still here.

12 **Another Problem** Some kids
13 hide food in their desks and
14 sneak nibbles when our teacher
15 isn't looking. But this isn't right.
16 When kids get caught they feel
17 embarrassed. And the whole class
18 is distracted from what we're
19 doing. Plus, our teacher gets angry.

20 **A Solution** There's no need for
21 this disruption. There's certainly no
22 need for us to go hungry at school.
23 Nutritious foods make for better
24 learners. I propose having a snack
25 time—healthy foods only—every
26 morning at 10:45. I think we all
27 will benefit from it.

Healthy Snacks

- Fresh fruits
- Dried fruits
- Granola bar
- Nuts
- Raw veggies
- Rice cakes
- String cheese
- Trail mix
- Yogurt

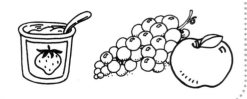

Name _____ Date _____

Bring Back Snacks

▶ **Answer each question. Give evidence from the essay.**

1 Which of the following is NOT a reason the writer gives for adding a snack time for third graders?

○ A. Snack time wastes work time.   ○ C. Hungry students can't focus on their work.

○ B. Third graders still get hungry.   ○ D. Students try to sneak snacks in their desks.

What in the text helped you answer? _____

_____

2 A person who is *famished* (line 4) would most long for _____.

○ A. a warm blanket   ○ C. books to read

○ B. something to eat   ○ D. a cozy nap

What in the text helped you answer? _____

_____

3 According to the writer, what makes third grade different from the grades before?

_____

4 How does giving a list of snacks help the writer's argument? _____

_____

_____

5 Why does the writer discuss a second problem: hiding food in desks? Explain.

_____

_____

_____

Name _____ Date _____

Endurance Sports

What makes endurance sports so challenging?

1   **Triathlon** Most people
2   know how it feels to swim,
3   ride a bike, or run, and then
4   stop to rest. Some people do
5   all three—in a row! This kind
6   of race is called a triathlon.
7   In an official *triathlon*,
8   athletes swim about $\frac{1}{2}$ mile,
9   cycle 12 miles, and then run
10 about 3 miles.

11 **Triathletes** Triathletes must train long and hard to get their
12 bodies strong enough to do all three sports without stopping.
13 They must develop endurance for such a difficult race.

14 **Other Triathlons** The *Ironman* is a harder triathlon. In it,
15 athletes swim almost $2\frac{1}{2}$ miles, cycle 112 miles, and then run
16 over 26 miles! The *Ultraman* triathlon is more demanding still.
17 The distances for each part are much greater.

18 **Unique Triathlete** As you can imagine, endurance events
19 challenge even the finest athletes. This is why Jason Lester is so
20 amazing. "If you don't stop, you can't be stopped," says Lester.
21 He is someone who truly knows what he's talking about.
22   When Jason was 12 years old, he was badly hurt
23 in a car accident. He suffered many injuries. Among
24 them was a **paralyzed** right arm. But his disability

paralyzed
unable to feel
or move part
of the body

25 didn't stop him. Jason competes successfully in both
26 *Ironman* and *Ultraman* triathlons. And he does it
27 without the use of one arm!

Name _____ Date _____

Endurance Sports

▶ **Answer each question. Give evidence from the article.**

1 Which of these athletic contests is the MOST challenging?

○ A. a half triathlon   ○ C. an *Ultraman* triathlon

○ B. an official triathlon   ○ D. an *Ironman* triathlon

What in the text helped you answer? _____

_____

_____

2 Which of the following words helps tell you the number of events in a *triathlon* race?

○ A. trial   ○ B. triangle   ○ C. trickled   ○ D. trimming

How did you choose your answer? _____

_____

3 What does it mean to have great *endurance*? Consult a dictionary, as needed.

_____

_____

4 Why does the author state that Jason "truly knows what he's talking about" (line 21)?

_____

_____

5 Many people compete in endurance sports. Why do you think the author decided to include Jason Lester in this article? Explain.

_____

_____

Name _____ Date _____

A Well-Rounded Person

How have Dr. Jemison's experiences shaped her life?

1   Mae Jemison is a doctor and researcher. She
2   served in the Peace Corps for two years. In addition
3   to English, she speaks Russian, Japanese, and
4   Swahili. She is a trained dancer, choreographer,
5   and actor. She has appeared on TV many times.
6   She also runs her own business.

7   But most Americans know her for another
8   reason. Dr. Jemison is an astronaut. Jemison was
9   the first African American woman to travel into
10 space. She did this in 1992 as a crew member on
11 the Space Shuttle Endeavor.

12   You can learn a lot about a person from
13 reading her exact words.

Peace Corps
U.S. government agency that sends trained volunteers to help improve living conditions in poor countries of the world

Swahili
language spoken in eastern Africa

14 *Space and its resources*
15 *belong to all of us, not*
16 *to any one group.*

17 *Science is very important*
18 *to me, but I also like to*
19 *stress that you have to be*
20 *well-rounded. One's love*
21 *for science doesn't get rid*
22 *of the other areas. I truly*
23 *feel someone interested*
24 *in science is interested*
25 *in understanding what's*
26 *going on in the world.*

Astronaut Mae Jemison

27 *The thing that*
28 *I have done*
29 *throughout my*
30 *life is to do the*
31 *best job that I can*
32 *and to be me.*

33 *Don't let*
34 *anyone rob*
35 *you of your*
36 *imagination,*
37 *your creativity,*
38 *or your*
39 *curiosity.*

Name _____ Date _____

A Well-Rounded Person

▶ **Answer each question. Give evidence from the biography.**

1 What is Swahili?

○ A. a business   ○ C. an African language

○ B. a kind of dance   ○ D. a government agency

What in the text helped you answer? _____

_____

2 Which of the following is Dr. Jemison best known for?

○ A. She is a trained dancer.

○ B. She has appeared many times on TV.

○ C. She served in the Peace Corps for two years.

○ D. She was the first African American woman to go into space.

What in the text helped you answer? _____

_____

3 What does Dr. Jemison believe should be important to scientists? _____

_____

4 Find words that Dr. Jemison has said to support the idea that people should never let go of their dreams.

_____

_____

5 What does it mean to be a person who is *well-rounded* (line 20)? _____

_____

Name _____ Date _____

Describing a Dollar

How do the photo and text work together to give information?

1 The United States prints paper money of different values.
2 Each bill states its value in words and numbers. Designs,
3 symbols, and pictures add detail and beauty to the bills.
4 Look closely at the front of a dollar.

Legal tender means that this official money must be accepted as payment.

Words give the full name of our **country**.

The **numbers** in each corner tell the bill's value in dollars.

The **black seal** shows which Federal Reserve Bank ordered the bill to be printed.

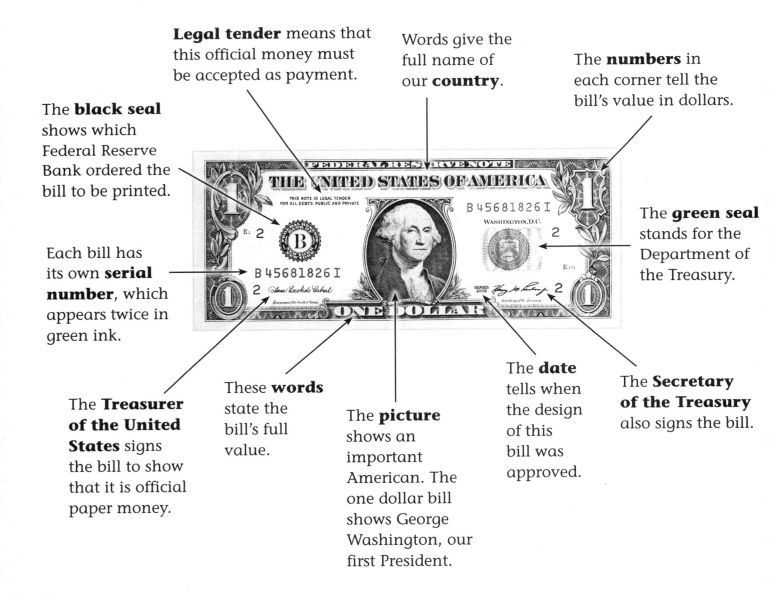

The **green seal** stands for the Department of the Treasury.

Each bill has its own **serial number**, which appears twice in green ink.

The **Treasurer of the United States** signs the bill to show that it is official paper money.

These **words** state the bill's full value.

The **picture** shows an important American. The one dollar bill shows George Washington, our first President.

The **date** tells when the design of this bill was approved.

The **Secretary of the Treasury** also signs the bill.

Name _____ Date _____

Describing a Dollar

▶ **Answer each question. Give evidence from the photo and captions.**

1 Which of these appears *twice* on the front of a dollar bill?

⚪ A. the serial number   ⚪ C. the picture of a famous American

⚪ B. the value of the bill   ⚪ D. the name of the Secretary of the Treasury

What in the text helped you answer? _____

_____

2 Which is most likely a job for the U.S. Treasury Department?

⚪ A. to search for buried treasure   ⚪ C. to run the Army, Navy, and Air Force

⚪ B. to run public schools and libraries   ⚪ D. to be in charge of the nation's money

What in the text helped you answer? _____

_____

3 What is the meaning of the term *legal tender*? _____

_____

4 Look carefully at the front of the dollar bill. How many times does its value appear?
Explain.

_____

5 Describe the front of a dollar bill as if to someone who has never seen one.
Include many clear details in your paragraph.

_____

_____

_____

_____

Name _____ Date _____

A Prickly Idea

How did an annoying problem lead to a clever idea?

1 **Hiking** In 1948, George de Mestral
2 was hiking in the Swiss Alps. He was
3 irritated by all the burrs that stuck
4 to his pants and socks. These prickly,
5 clinging seed cases were annoying.
6 They were hard to pull off. But they
7 gave him an idea. De Mestral, an
8 engineer, wondered if he could make
9 an imitation burr. Maybe it could
10 compete with the zipper as a way to
11 fasten clothing and other things. So he
12 got busy.

Clump of burrs

13 **Inventing** He worked on his idea
14 for several years. Eventually, he
15 produced two cotton strips—one
16 covered with tiny hooks and the
17 other covered with tiny loops. These
18 fabric strips stuck together and
19 stayed that way until pulled apart.
20 De Mestral called his invention
21 *locking tape.* He then improved his
22 idea by using sturdy nylon instead
23 of cotton.

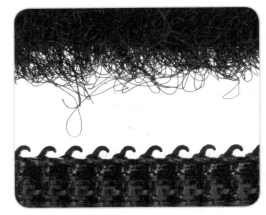

Close-up of the hooks and loops
of Velcro®

24 **Naming** Next, de Mestral formed a company to produce his
25 hook-and-loop fastener. He called the product Velcro. He chose *vel*
26 because he liked the sound of the word *velvet.* He picked *cro* from
27 the French word *crochet,* a hook.

28 **Lasting** Today, Velcro products and similar fasteners are used
29 around the world. And it all started with some bothersome burrs.

Name _____ Date _____

A Prickly Idea

▶ **Answer each question. Give evidence from the article.**

1 What are *burrs* (line 3)?

    ○ A. clinging seed cases   ○ C. types of fabric

    ○ B. pants and socks   ○ D. kinds of tape

What in the text helped you answer? _____

_____

2 Which of the following expressions might make another good title for this article?

    ○ A. Go Take a Hike!   ○ C. Burrs Under My Saddle

    ○ B. A Happy Accident   ○ D. Accidentally on Purpose

What in the text helped you answer? _____

_____

_____

3 Explain the meaning of de Mestral's first name for his new invention, *locking tape* (line 21).

_____

_____

4 What features of burrs gave de Mestral a big idea? _____

_____

5 Based on this article, describe George de Mestral's character. _____

_____

_____

_____

Name _____ Date _____

Make Sense

In what ways does the title fit this essay?

1   Suppose a child wakes up sneezing. She whines and begs to go
2   to the hospital. Her dad takes her temperature, but it is normal.
3   He checks her eyes and throat, but they seem normal, too. Still, the
4   child insists that she needs emergency care.
5   Annoyed, her dad says, "Honey,
6   *don't make a mountain out of a mole*
7   *hill!*" His message is that she is
8   making a huge fuss over something
9   that is minor. He used an **idiom** that
10 contrasts an enormous mountain with
11 a tiny mole hill to make his point.

12 Can a ghost story *make your hair*
13 *stand on end*? This idiom means that
14 you feel really scared. It comes from
15 the scientific fact that when people or
16 animals feel fear, their muscles get tight,
17 and the hair on their bodies actually
18 seems to stand up stiffly. You can see
19 cats do this when they are frightened.

20 Do delicious treats *make your mouth*
21 *water*? This idiom also comes from science.
22 The mouth gives off a juicy fluid known as
23 *saliva*. Saliva is mostly water. It helps you
24 swallow and digest foods you eat. So, this
25 idiom suggests that you can almost taste
26 the food even before it gets in your mouth.

Name _____ Date _____

Make Sense

▶ **Answer each question. Give evidence from the essay.**

1 Which word is opposite in meaning to *minor* (line 9)?

○ A. major   ○ B. small   ○ C. heavy   ○ D. normal

What in the text helped you answer? _____

_____

2 Which is mostly likely to *make your mouth water* (lines 20 and 21)?

○ A. watching a scary movie   ○ C. making a fuss

○ B. smelling a pie baking   ○ D. sneezing

What in the text helped you answer? _____

_____

3 What are some other phrases you might use that mean the same as *make your hair stand on end* (lines 12 and 13)?

_____

_____

_____

4 When I offer my dog a treat, she licks her lips before she tastes it. Which of the three idioms is closest in meaning to this?

_____

5 Here's another idiom with the word *make*: Alysse can never *make up her mind!* Explain what this might mean about Alysse.

_____

_____

Name _____ Date _____

Hot-Air Balloon Ride

How would you describe Clay's hot-air balloon experience?

1 June 12, 2013

2 Dear Grandma,

3   Mom didn't want to worry you,
4 but now that we're safely on the
5 ground, I can tell you about our
6 hot-air balloon ride.

7   At dawn, we climbed up into a
8 large square wicker basket, where
9 the pilot, Todd, was waiting. It
10 was nippy, and we were wearing
11 layers because that's what was
12 recommended in the brochure. We
13 were really excited.

Someone on the ground took this photo of us up in the balloon!

14   Then Todd talked to us. Pointing
15 to our brightly colored balloon, he
16 said that it was the size of 90,000
17 soccer balls. He said it rose by
18 adding heat and descended by releasing heat. Then Todd showed us
19 his instruments: an *altimeter* for measuring height, a *variometer* for
20 measuring climbing and descending speeds, and a fuel gauge. The fuel
21 that made heat was liquid propane—like we use in our backyard grill.

22   *Suddenly,* we were aloft. We floated, as if in a cloud. And, heated
23 by the flame, we began to peel off layers. The higher we soared, the
24 more magnificent the views. But we weren't exactly drifting silently;
25 the burner noise was deafening and constant. Poor Marcy held her
26 ears and, in addition, was too short to enjoy the views. Dad had to
27 hold her up. But I had earplugs and felt like I was in *The Wizard of Oz.*

28 Love you,

29 Clay

Name _____ Date _____

Hot-Air Balloon Ride

▶ **Answer each question. Give evidence from the letter.**

1 Which is used to measure climbing speed?

○ A. propane   ○ B. fuel gauge   ○ C. altimeter   ○ D. variometer

How did you pick your answer? _____

_____

2 Which has about the same meaning as *recommended* (line 12)?

○ A. discouraged   ○ B. suggested   ○ C. required   ○ D. necessary

What in the text helped you answer? _____

_____

3 Who controlled the balloon's flight? _____

_____

4 Why might you suppose that Clay had a better time on the ride than Marcy did?

_____

_____

5 What details about the hot-air balloon flight did Clay leave out? List as many examples as you can.

_____

_____

_____

_____

Name _____ Date _____

Native American Gifts

Why does the writer link history and food?

1 **First Foods** People need food to survive. The first people who
2 lived in what is now the United States had different ways to get
3 food than we do today. These Native Americans hunted for meat
4 from animals, birds, and fish. They gathered roots, berries, nuts,
5 and grains to eat. They learned to use wild rice and sunflower
6 seeds. Over time, they grew crops, such as beans, melons,
7 peanuts, peppers, pumpkins, and squash. These are all foods we
8 eat to this day.

9 **Gratitude** We owe thanks to Native Americans for teaching us
10 about corn. For many groups, it was their most important
11 crop. First known as *maize*, corn today is the most
12 produced grain in all the world. Together, the world's
13 farmers produce nearly one billion tons of it a year.
14 That's a lot of corn!

15 **CORNucopia!** A *cornucopia* is a symbol of plenty.
16 You'd be amazed at the number of things we eat
17 or use that come from corn. Of course, everyone
18 knows about popcorn, corn muffins, or corn on the
19 cob. The table below shows some of the thousands
20 of other uses for corn.

A cornucopia is a
horn-shaped basket.

Common Products From Some Form of Corn

EDIBLE		NOT EDIBLE	
Breakfast cereals	Jam	Batteries	Makeup
Candies	Marshmallows	Candles	Paints
Cooking oil	Pancake mix	Cardboard	Rubber tires
Flour	Salad dressings	Charcoal	Shampoo
Grits	Vinegar	Disposable diapers	Shoe polish
Ice cream		Glue	

Name _____ Date _____

Native American Gifts

▶ **Answer each question. Give evidence from the essay.**

1 What is another word for *maize* (line 11)?

○ A. basket　　　　○ B. grain　　　　○ C. crop　　　　○ D. corn

What in the text helped you answer? _____

_____

_____

2 Which of the following corn products is NOT edible?

○ A. vinegar　　　○ B. charcoal　　　○ C. cooking oil　　　○ D. pancake mix

What in the text helped you answer? _____

_____

_____

3 Look at the picture. Why is a cornucopia also known as a *horn of plenty*? _____

_____

_____

4 Look at the chart. Explain the meaning of the word *edible*. _____

_____

_____

5 What is the main idea of this essay? _____

_____

_____

Name _____ Date _____

Parts of a Whale

How do the picture and text together help you understand the whale?

1 Like most other living creatures, whales have changed over
2 time to adapt to their environment. These magnificent marine
3 mammals spend their entire lives in oceans. Their sleek bodies
4 are perfect for long and deep dives. The way they breathe allows
5 them to stay underwater for more than an hour! Whales' tails
6 help them power through the water.
7 A sperm whale is a common kind of whale. Read about some
8 features of its large body.

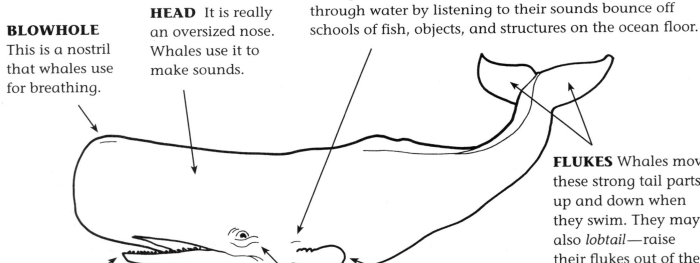

EARS Whales hear very well. They communicate through clicks, whistles, and songs. They navigate through water by listening to their sounds bounce off schools of fish, objects, and structures on the ocean floor.

HEAD It is really an oversized nose. Whales use it to make sounds.

BLOWHOLE This is a nostril that whales use for breathing.

FLUKES Whales move these strong tail parts up and down when they swim. They may also *lobtail*—raise their flukes out of the water into the air, and then slap them down on the water's surface with a loud smack. This might be another way whales communicate.

FLIPPERS These help whales steer themselves through the water.

TEETH Some whales have none, and feed by straining huge gulps of water. Others, like the sperm whale, have teeth and use them to grab prey.

EYES These are small because whales rely more on sounds to move and hunt.

Name _____ Date _____

Parts of a Whale

▶ **Answer each question. Give evidence from the diagram and captions.**

1 *Marine* mammals (lines 2 and 3) live in _____.

○ A. Alaska   ○ B. ponds   ○ C. rivers   ○ D. oceans

What in the text help you answer? _____

_____

2 Which of the following means about the same as *navigate*?

○ A. breathe   ○ B. swim quickly   ○ C. steer   ○ D. communicate

What in the text helped you answer? _____

_____

3 Why is it important for whales to have sleek bodies? _____

_____

_____

4 How can such a huge animal manage with such small eyes? _____

_____

_____

5 Compare and contrast the *flukes* and *flippers* of the sperm whale.
Include their use and location on the body in your answer.

_____

_____

_____

_____

Name _____ Date _____

Eagle or Turkey?

Why did Ben Franklin prefer the turkey?

1   **National Symbols** Countries often adopt animals as symbols.
2   England has its lion. Russia has its bear. We in America have
3   our bald eagle. Our lawmakers approved this impressive, fierce-
4   looking bird for our National Bird in 1782. They valued the
5   eagle's great strength and long life. But it was a controversial
6   choice. Benjamin Franklin was among those who disagreed with
7   the vote.

8   **Dishonest Bird**
9   The famous statesman,
10   inventor, and thinker was
11   critical of the decision
12   because he held a low
13   opinion of that bird.
14   Franklin wrote that the
15   eagle had a "bad moral

16   character" and that it got its living dishonestly. He explained that
17   the huge bird was too lazy to fish. Instead, he said, it would wait
18   for the hard-working fishing hawk to catch one. When the eagle
19   saw this happen, it would swoop down and snatch the fish away.

20   **Valiant Bird** The turkey, on the
21   other hand, was a more appropriate
22   national symbol, Franklin believed.
23   He conceded that this bird was "a
24   little vain and silly," but that it was
25   respectable and courageous. He
26   claimed that it wouldn't hesitate to
27   attack any red-coated British soldier
28   invading its barnyard.

Name _____ Date _____

Eagle or Turkey?

▶ **Answer each question. Give evidence from the anecdote.**

1 A *valiant* (line 20) bird would be _____.

○ A. vain   ○ B. brave   ○ C. honest   ○ D. cowardly

What in the text helped you answer? _____

_____

2 Which of the following was true about the decision to make the eagle
our national bird?

○ A. Everyone agreed on the eagle.   ○ C. Not everybody agreed with the choice.

○ B. Most people preferred the bear.   ○ D. Only Ben Franklin disagreed with the choice.

What in the text helped you answer? _____

_____

3 Contrast the eagle and the turkey based on the pictures. _____

_____

_____

4 Why did Ben Franklin write that the eagle had a "bad moral character" (lines 15 and 16)?

_____

_____

5 Was Franklin being serious about the National Bird, or was he joking?
Support your idea with text details.

_____

_____

_____

Literature Passages

Passage 1: Kadimba's Field

1. B; Sample answer: I read that Kadimba was lazy and hated work (lines 1–2). He probably didn't look forward to the huge job. **2.** C; Sample answer: Kadimba fooled Elephant and Hippo into thinking they were going to have a tug-of-war with him but really he was tricking them into clearing all the bushes so he could plant his crops (lines 5–7, 12–14, 16–28). **3.** Sample answer: They didn't know about Kadimba's trick. Each one expected the tug-of-war against the small hare to end quickly with himself as an easy winner (lines 7–15). **4.** Sample answer: He had to wait for another strong animal to come along and play tug-of-war against Elephant (lines 12–14). **5.** Sample answer: Clearing the field was hard for a hare, but easy for big strong animals. So, he planned a way to trick Elephant and Hippo to compete and clear the field without realizing it (lines 5–6, 16–28).

Passage 2: Follow Me

1. B; Sample answer: I read, "We scrambled down," so I picked B (lines 18–19). **2.** A; Sample answer: Mimi says that they will enter a tunnel made by lava (lines 14–17). **3.** Sample answer: It sounds like Mimi must have been there before and knows that it is dark in a lava tube, so she came prepared (lines 1–3, 8–17). **4.** Sample answer: It's dark, slippery, narrow, silent, and unfamiliar (lines 18–26). **5.** Sample answer: I think it means that the tunnel was getting smaller and smaller. They stopped and turned back probably because there wasn't room to go farther (lines 23–26).

Passage 3: A "Punny" Pair

1. B; Sample answer: The first sentence talks about a powerful enemy. So, it sounds like the castle and the people inside were being attacked and couldn't fight off the enemy (lines 1–8). **2.** C; Sample answer: The joke is about needing one dollar to go to the movies, so I think a *greenback* is a dollar bill (lines 23–28).

3. Sample answer: He has to send a knight for help, but has no horses for the knight to ride (lines 1–8). **4.** Sample answer: In real life, animals don't go to the movies or need money (lines 20–25). Also, the ending is funny (lines 26–28). **5.** Sample answer: Both jokes are funny because they use words that sound alike but have different meanings, and the first one also switches the order of words to make it funny (lines 18, 26–28).

Passage 4: One Clever Cat

1. D; Sample answer: I read that Tiger looked up in fear when Lupe came in (lines 1–3). Also, Tiger wriggled, squirmed, fidgeted, and ran away from her, so I think that Tiger was scared and nervous around Lupe (lines 6–11). **2.** B; Sample answer: Lupe was dressed up when she got to Inez's house, and Inez invited her to choose a necklace (lines 6–8, 13). **3.** Sample answer: Tiger was a clever cat because she found a good hiding place where Lupe couldn't find her (lines 18–23). Inez also calls her a "smart kitten," and *smart* means the same thing as *clever* (line 26). **4.** Sample answer: Tiger was relieved that Lupe was gone (lines 23–25). **5.** Sample answer: I think Inez knew that Tiger didn't like to be handled by Lupe, but she would never say that to Lupe because it would hurt her feelings (lines 18–28).

Passage 5: Fishing on the Rogue

1. C; Sample answer: The story is about fishing, and people haul them in, so it must be a type of fish (lines 1–5, 14–15). **2.** C; Sample answer: I read that fishing is one of the few things to do there in the rainy season, so I figured that people fish from a truck to keep dry (lines 5–13). **3.** Sample answer: It's in winter (line 18). **4.** Sample answer: It looks like a beach or sandbar along both edges of a river, but it's rocky instead of sandy (photo). **5.** Sample answer: It uses folksy words, like *That there is, There's one over yonder!* and *We set there* (lines 1, 10, 12), exaggeration (lines 16–17), silliness (lines 9–13), and it tells a goofy story (lines 15–17).

Passage 6: The Crow and the Pitcher

1. C; Sample answer: I read that the crow was feverish from thirst (lines 1–2). **2.** D; Sample answer: It says the crow couldn't reach the water because the neck was too narrow (lines 7–10). So, I looked at the picture and saw the place on the pitcher that was too small for the crow's beak to fit in. **3.** Sample answer: The crow is very thirsty and finds some water, but she can't reach the water (lines 7–15). **4.** Sample answer: The heavy pebbles fall to the bottom and take up space, and lift the water up (lines 18–24). **5.** Sample answer: Sometimes the way to solve a big problem is to take small steps. That's what the crow did (lines 17–24).

Passage 7: Norse All-Father

1. A; Sample answer: I read that Asgard was where Odin's silver palace was (lines 5–6). **2.** C; Sample answer: I read all four choices. I found A (line 1), B (lines 9–10, 21, 24–26), and D (line 3) in the story. I read that Odin could smother fire (lines 13–15), but it didn't say he could make it, so I picked C. **3.** Sample answer: Odin's voice was very soft, which made people believe he was always telling the truth (lines 22–24). **4.** (Answers will vary. Accept any two reasonable synonyms.) Sample answers: *Look, see,* or *stare.* **5.** Sample answer: Odin always tried to gather as much information about the world as he could. He knew what was happening everywhere and where all the treasures were, and he used it to his advantage (lines 9–10, 15–17, 21, 24–26).

Passage 8: The Mirror Stirs

1. B; Sample answer: I read each choice, reread the passage, and looked at the photo (lines 4–12). **2.** D; The town was lonely and old. The schoolhouse was just a skeleton now, and there were only remains of the jail (lines 4–12). So, I think a ghost town is most like D. **3.** Sample answer: I read that they were both panting (out of breath) and sweaty when they got to their parents. So, I bet they ran as fast as they could because they were scared! (lines 24–26) **4.** Sample answer: Wyatt the dog was probably behind it cooling off. When he moved, the mirror moved (lines 21–23, 28–30). **5.** Sample answer:

Calling the old schoolhouse a skeleton sounds like it is just part of a building—only its frame, which is like the bones of a skeleton. Also, the town was dead and lonely—a ghost town (lines 4–12, 15–17).

Passage 9: A New House

1. A; Sample answer: The person telling the story talks about Pa, Silas, and Ma. I also read the part that said, "Ma and I set to cooking," so I knew it was Jenny (lines 7–10). **2.** B; Sample answer: The story says that they went to get boards, pegs, and a plow. You can call those things "building supplies" (lines 8–9). **3.** Sample answer: Sod is grass and the ground it grows in (lines 8–9). **4.** Sample answer: The walls are made of thick sod bricks cut by Pa and Silas from the ground itself (lines 14–19). They left space to add a door and a window (lines 21–28). **5.** Sample answer: I read that the lean-to was for shelter. They knew it would take time to build a house and needed a place to live until then (lines 7–10).

Informational Text Passages

Passage 10: Gary's Tuba

1. C; Sample answer: Gary says that the tuba is made of brass (line 4). Later he says it's the biggest instrument in the brass family (lines 8–9). **2.** B; Sample answer: I read all the choices, and found that B is the only fact that isn't true. The tuba is the biggest brass instrument, but not the biggest instrument (lines 8–9). **3.** Sample answer: I found the bell. Its name makes sense because it is shaped like a bell, and it's where the sound comes out (lines 14–15). **4.** Sample answer: I read that the tuba weighs 30 pounds, which is a lot! And you need to be able to suck in a lot of air. So, it probably makes sense for kids to start after they've grown bigger and stronger (lines 5, 17–18). **5.** Sample answer: I think the interviewer knows that the tuba makes a very loud and deep sound and wonders how that feels to the player.

Passage 11: Wash and Dry

1. D; Sample answer: The first paragraph says *Welcome to Lucy's Do-It-Yourself Laundry*, so I picked D (line 1). **2.** B; Sample answer: I read the list of WASH steps and compared it to the choices. B is what you do first (lines 5–16). **3.** Sample answer: It takes about 30 minutes (line 14). **4.** Sample answer: It costs $2.00. I looked at the Price List. It's $1.25 for the wash, plus 3 quarters for the 30 minutes in the dryer (Price List). **5.** Sample answer: I think there are more things to do to get a load ready for the washer. You have to sort it and add soap (lines 5–15).

Passage 12: Hello, Roy G. Biv!

1. B; Sample answer: I reread the paragraph about rainbows and about the prism. The article says you cannot touch a rainbow, so I picked B (lines 5–10, sidebar). **2.** A; Sample answer: I read that *refracted* means *bent* (lines 25–27). **3.** Sample answer: There is no such person. "Roy G. Biv" is a shortcut way to help you remember the colors of the spectrum in order: red, orange, yellow, green, blue, indigo, violet (sidebar). **4.** Sample answer: Newton was a famous scientist who discovered important ideas about light that we still use today (lines 12–31). **5.** Sample answer: I think the author wanted to get readers interested right away in something that is well known to them. And it is a great way to start talking about rainbows (lines 1–4).

Passage 13: Multiple Meanings

1. D; Sample answer: I counted the number of different meanings. There are six (line 24). **2.** A; Sample answer: I read all the choices. Only A wasn't in the dictionary entry, so I picked it (lines 10–25). **3.** Sample answer: I think it is meaning 4. In that meaning and in the sentence, *plot* is used in the same way (lines 20–21). **4.** Sample answer: The "entry word" is the word that is going to be defined (line 10). **5.** Sample answer: I think it is meaning 5—"to make a map or diagram." These people will probably look at a map to plan the route they will take to the beach (lines 22–23).

Passage 14: Healthy and Crispy

1. D; Sample answer: I read each choice and checked to find it in the text. The only one that isn't there is D (lines 1–3). **2.** A; Sample answer: Step 2 talks about toasting the seeds in a pan, so I know they are getting heated. Then it says, "Don't let them scorch." So, I think *scorch* is another word for *burn*. I know that when toast burns, it gets dark brown. That's why I picked A (lines 18–19). **3.** Sample answer: You could collect the ingredients and utensils in any order as long as you have them all before you start. But you have to follow the preparation and cooking steps in order. **4.** Sample answer: I think it's because you shouldn't even start cooking until you have gathered everything you need. **5.** Sample answer: The ingredients list includes butter, sugar, an egg, and flour, which are used to make many kinds of cookies (lines 9–12); the first utensil is a cookie sheet; and step 5 talks about a cookie sheet, then says the dough spreads out as it bakes, like a lot of cookies do (lines 23–24).

Passage 15: Place Names

1. C; Sample answer: A fossil is from an extinct animal or plant. I picked C, thinking that fossils were found at that place, just like Dinosaur, Colorado (lines 15–16). **2.** C; Sample answer: Of the four choices, the one that sounds most like someone's name is Eugene (lines 13–14). **3.** Sample answer: Both men moved from the East and settled in the same place in Oregon in 1845. They decided its name by a coin toss—Portland (lines 1–6). **4.** Sample answers might include: Seaside, Gold Beach, Oakridge, Klamath Falls, Canyonville (lines 11–12). **5.** Sample answer: Grant is probably the name of someone famous or a person who lived there or did something important there. A pass might be a way to travel between mountains (lines 11–14).

Passage 16: Bring Back Snacks

1. A; Sample answer: I read each choice and only the first one isn't part of the writer's argument (lines 1–6, 10–15). **2.** B; Sample answer: The author talks about getting hungry during the morning at school (lines 1–6). **3.** Sample answer: In third grade there is no longer a snack time, but there was in the earlier grades (lines 7–10). **4.** Sample answer: The snacks listed remind readers that snacks can be healthy and good for you and don't have to be cooked (sidebar). **5.** Sample answer: I think the main problem is how to prevent hungry kids. But that problem also causes other problems; so, solving the first one would probably solve the other (lines 12–27).

Passage 17: Endurance Sports

1. C; Sample answer: I reread the parts about the three kinds of triathlons (lines 1–17). It says in line 16 that the Ultraman is the most demanding, so I picked C. **2.** B; Sample answer: If I didn't know how many events a triathlon had, the word *triangle* might help me guess "three" because a triangle has three sides and three angles. The other *tri-* words wouldn't help me since they are not number words. **3.** Sample answer: I think it means to have the energy, strength, and courage to keep going no matter what (lines 11–20). **4.** Sample answer: The author means that Jason might have stopped after he got hurt, but he didn't. So, this saying describes Jason very well (lines 22–27). **5.** Sample answer: Endurance sports demand a lot from any athlete. But Jason had to deal with his paralyzed right arm to be as good or better than others. He is a good example of someone who never gives up and keeps on going (lines 11–13, 18–27). And he could be an inspiration to others.

Passage 18: A Well-Rounded Person

1. C; Sample answer: The text at the side says that Swahili is a language in eastern Africa, and it appears in a sentence about the languages Dr. Jemison speaks (lines 2–4 and sidebar). **2.** D; Sample answer: The second paragraph says that most Americans know Dr. Jemison as an astronaut (lines 7–11). **3.** Sample answer: She says that scientists should be interested in understanding what's going on in the world (lines 22–26). **4.** Sample answer: I think that's what she means in the last quotation: "Don't let anyone rob you of your imagination, your creativity, or your curiosity" (lines 33–39). **5.** Sample answer:

A well-rounded person is someone who has many different interests and knows about many different things (lines 22–26).

Passage 19: Describing a Dollar

1. A; Sample answer: The text says that the serial number appears twice in green ink (serial number caption). **2.** D; Sample answer: I read all the choices, but only D makes sense with the photo and information. **3.** Sample answer: Legal tender means that this is official money and it must be accepted as payment (legal tender caption). **4.** Sample answer: Six times. I see four numeral *1*s, and I see the word *one* twice—once at the bottom and once behind the seal on the right (photo). **5.** Answers will vary; check for accurate and complete descriptions.

Passage 20: A Prickly Idea

1. A; Sample answer: The author defines burrs as "prickly, clinging seed cases" (lines 4–5). **2.** B; Sample answer: I picked B because the sticky burrs were an accident that led de Mestral to come up with a useful invention (lines 2–12). **3.** Sample answer: The *tape* means the two strips of fabric that will stick together; *locking* means that they stay stuck until you pull them apart (lines 14–19). **4.** Sample answer: When he saw how well the burrs clung and how hard they were to pull off, it made him think about a new idea for fastening clothing and other things (lines 6–12). **5.** Sample answer: I think he was a clever, creative, and hard-working person who used his education to come up with something new and useful (lines 6–25).

Passage 21: Make Sense

1. A; Sample answer: I know from the first story that *minor* is something little or not important. So, I picked A (lines 1–9). **2.** B; Sample answer: I reread the part about making your mouth water. The best choice is "smelling a pie baking" because its fantastic smell makes you think of eating (lines 20–26). **3.** Sample answer: You might say, *make you scared to death, make you terrified, frightened,* or *scared silly* (lines 12–14). **4.** Sample answer: It's most likely making her mouth water because it seems like she's getting ready to taste the food (lines 20–26). **5.** Sample answer: It might mean that Alysse has a hard time deciding.

Passage 22: Hot-Air Balloon Ride

1. D; Sample answer: I found each of those words in the passage and reread what they are. I read that the variometer measures climbing and descending speeds (lines 19–20). **2.** B; Sample answer: It said in the brochure that wearing warm clothes was recommended. That's probably because it would be cold up in the balloon. But it didn't say you had to wear them so C and D couldn't be right. And *discouraged* means the opposite, so A is not right either (lines 9–12). **3.** Sample answer: Todd did, because he was the pilot (lines 7–9). **4.** Sample answer: Clay had earplugs, so the noise didn't bother him so much, and he was tall enough to be able to see the great views. Marcy had to hold her ears and couldn't see the view without being lifted up (lines 24–27). **5.** (Answers will vary. Accept reasonable responses.) Sample answer: Clay didn't say where they flew from, how high they flew, how long the flight lasted, who else might have been in the basket with them, what they saw, how the landing was, or whether they would want to do it again one day.

Passage 23: Native American Gifts

1. D; Sample answer: The author writes that corn was first called *maize* (line 11). **2.** B; Sample answer: I read each choice and found it in the chart. Charcoal is in the NOT EDIBLE side. **3.** Sample answer: It's shaped like a horn and filled to overflowing with lots of food (picture and caption). **4.** Sample answer: It means things you can eat. When I look at the chart, all of the things in the EDIBLE column are foods. **5.** Sample answer: The main idea is that we should be grateful to Native Americans, who taught us a great deal about foods we still grow and eat today, especially corn (lines 9–20).

Passage 24: Parts of a Whale

1. D; Sample answer: The author says that whales spend their entire lives in oceans (lines 2–3). **2.** C; Sample answer: In the caption about ears, I read that whales "navigate through water by listening to their sounds." That makes me think they are finding their way as they move, so *steer* seems like the best answer. **3.** Sample answer: It helps them make long and deep dives (lines 3–4). **4.** Sample answer: I read that whales rely more on sounds than on sight to move and hunt (Eyes caption). **5.** Sample answer: The flukes are the tail at the back of the whale's body. The flippers are on the side of the body. The whale uses its flukes for power when swimming, and maybe to communicate with other whales. It uses its flippers to steer itself as it swims (Flukes and Flippers captions).

Passage 25: Eagle or Turkey?

1. B; Sample answer: I reread that paragraph, and saw that the turkey is courageous. That means about the same thing as *brave* (lines 20–25). **2.** C; Sample answer: The author says that the choice was controversial. That means that people disagreed about it (lines 5–7). **3.** (Answers will vary. Accept reasonable responses that are supported by the photos.) Sample answers: The eagle has a wide wingspan, but the turkey has a big fantail. The eagle has a small body with big wings so it can fly easily. The turkey's body looks very big, like it might be too heavy to fly well. **4.** Sample answer: I think it's because the eagle didn't catch its own food, but stole it from others (lines 16–19). **5.** (Answers may vary. Accept reasonable responses.) Sample answer 1: I think Ben Franklin was serious. He believed that the eagle set a bad example, and that the turkey had more honesty and character (lines 14–28). Sample answer 2: I think he must have been joking. The turkey is a funny-looking bird to have as a national symbol. Plus, the part about the turkey attacking a British soldier is funny, too (lines 25–28).

25 Complex Text Passages to Meet the Common Core: Literature and Informational Texts, Grade 3 © 2014 by Scholastic Teaching Resources